ALAIN DE BOTTON

The News

Alain de Botton is the author of essays on themes rang-
ing from love and travel to architecture and philosophy.
His bestselling books include *How Proust Can Change
Your Life*, *The Art of Travel*, and *The Architecture of Happiness*. He lives in London, where he is the founder and
chairman of The School of Life (www.theschooloflife.
com) and the creative director of Living Architecture
(www.living-architecture.co.uk).

INTERNATIONAL

Also by Alain de Botton

Essays in Love
How Proust Can Change Your Life
The Consolations of Philosophy
The Art of Travel
Status Anxiety
The Architecture of Happiness
The Pleasures and Sorrows of Work
A Week at the Airport
Religion for Atheists
How to Think More about Sex
Art as Therapy

The News

The News
A User's Manual

ALAIN DE BOTTON

Vintage International
Vintage Books
A Division of Random House LLC
New York

FIRST VINTAGE INTERNATIONAL EDITION, DECEMBER 2014

Grateful acknowledgment is made to New Directions Publishing Corp.
and Carcanet Press Limited for permission to reprint from "Asphodel, That
Greeny Flower" by William Carlos Williams from *The Collected Poems:
Volume II, 1939–1962,* copyright © 1944 by William Carlos Williams.
Reprinted by permission of New Directions Publishing Corp. and
Carcanet Press Limited.

The Library of Congress has cataloged the Pantheon edition as follows:
De Botton, Alain.
The news : a user's manual / Alain de Botton.
p. cm.
1. Journalism—Social aspects. 2. Journalism—Political aspects.
3. Mass media—Social aspects. 4. Mass media—Political aspects.
5. News audiences. I. Title.
PN4749.D43 2014 302.23—dc23 2013031206

Vintage Trade Paperback ISBN: 978-0-307-47683-8
eBook ISBN: 978-0-307-91172-8

Book design by Katrina Wiedner

www.vintagebooks.com

Printed in the United States of America
10 9 8 7 6 5 4 3

For my mother

Contents

I.

Preface

I.

IT DOESN'T COME with any instructions, because it's meant to be the most normal, easy, obvious and unremarkable activity in the world, like breathing or blinking.

After an interval, usually no longer than a night (and often far less; if we're feeling particularly restless, we might only manage ten or fifteen minutes), we interrupt whatever we are doing in order to *check the news*. We put our lives on hold in the expectation of receiving yet another dose of critical information about all the most significant achievements, catastrophes, crimes, epidemics and romantic complications to have befallen mankind anywhere around the planet since we last had a look.

What follows is an exercise in trying to make this ubiquitous and familiar habit seem a lot weirder and rather more hazardous than it does at present.

2.

THE NEWS IS committed to laying before us whatever is supposed to be most unusual and important in the world: a snowfall in the tropics; a love child for the president; a set of conjoined twins. Yet for all its determined pursuit of the anomalous, the one thing the news skilfully avoids training its eye on is itself, and the predominant position it has achieved in our lives. 'Half of Humanity Daily Spellbound by the News' is a headline we are never likely to see from organizations otherwise devoted to the remarkable and the noteworthy, the corrupt and the shocking.

Societies become modern, the philosopher Hegel suggested, when news replaces religion as our central source of guidance and our touchstone of authority. In the developed economies, the news now occupies a position of power at least equal to that formerly enjoyed by the faiths. Dispatches track the canonical hours with uncanny precision: matins have been transubstantiated into the breakfast bulletin, vespers into the evening report. But the news doesn't just follow a quasi-religious timetable. It also demands that we approach it with some of the same deferential expectations we would once have harboured of the faiths. Here, too, we hope to receive revelations, learn who is good and bad, fathom suffering and understand the unfolding logic of existence. And here, too, if we refuse to take part in the rituals, there could be imputations of heresy.

The news knows how to render its own mechanics almost invisible and therefore hard to question. It speaks to us in a natural unaccented voice, without reference to its own assumption-laden perspective. It fails to disclose that it does not merely *report* on the world, but is instead constantly at work crafting a new planet in our minds in line with its own often highly distinctive priorities.

3.

FROM AN EARLY age, we are educated to appreciate the power of images and words. We are led to museums and solemnly informed that certain pictures by long-dead artists could transform our perspectives. We are introduced to poems and stories that might change our lives.

Yet, oddly, people seldom attempt to educate us about the words and images proffered to us every hour by the news. It is deemed more important for us to know how to make sense of the plot of *Othello* than how to decode the front page of the *New York Post*. We are more likely to hear about the significance of Matisse's use of colour than to be taken through the effects of the celebrity photo section of the *Daily Mail*. We aren't encouraged to consider what might happen to our outlooks after immersion in *Bild* or *OK!* magazine, the *Frankfurter Allgemeine Zeitung* or the *Hokkaido Shimbun*, the *Tehran Times* or the *Sun*. We are never systematically inducted into the extraordinary capacity of news outlets to influence our sense of reality and to mould the state of what we might as well – with no supernatural associations – call our souls.

For all their talk of education, modern societies neglect to examine by far the most influential means by which their populations are educated. Whatever happens in our classrooms, the more potent and ongoing kind of education takes place on the airwaves and on our screens. Cocooned in classrooms for only our first eighteen years or so, we effectively spend the rest of our lives under the tutelage of news entities which wield infinitely greater influence over us than any academic institution can. Once our formal education has finished, the news is the teacher. It is the single most significant force setting the tone of public life and shaping our impressions of the community beyond our own walls. It is the prime creator of political and social reality. As revolutionaries well know, if you want to change the mentality of a country, you don't head to the art gallery, the department of education or the homes of famous novelists; you drive the tanks straight to the nerve centre of the body politic, the news HQ.

4.

WHY DO WE, the audience, keep checking the news? Dread has a lot to do with it. After even a short period of being cut off from news, our apprehensions have a habit of accumulating. We know how much is liable to go wrong and how fast: an A380 may rupture its fuel line and cartwheel into the bay in flames, a virus from an African bat may leap the species barrier and infiltrate the air vents of a crowded Japanese commuter train, investors may precipitate a run on the currency and yet another deceptively ordinary father may call a violent end to the lives of his two beautiful young children.

In the immediate vicinity, there might well be stability and peace. In the garden, a breeze may be swaying the branches of the plum tree and dust may slowly be gathering on the bookshelves in the living room. But we are aware that such serenity does not do justice to the chaotic and violent fundamentals of existence and hence, after a time, it has a habit of growing worrisome in its own way. Our background awareness of the possibility of catastrophe explains the small pulse of fear we may register when we angle our phones in the direction of the nearest mast and wait for the headlines to appear. It is a version of the apprehension that our distant ancestors must have felt in the chill moments before dawn, as they wondered whether the sun would ever find its way back into the firmament.

Yet there is a particular kind of pleasure at stake here, too. The news, however dire it may be and perhaps especially when it is at its worst, can come as a relief from the claustrophobic burden of living with ourselves, of forever trying to do justice to our own potential and of struggling to persuade a few people in our limited orbit to take our ideas and needs seriously. To consult the news is to raise a seashell to our ears and to be overpowered by the roar of humanity. It can be an escape from our preoccupations to locate issues that are so much graver and more compelling than those we have been uniquely allotted, and to allow these larger concerns to drown out our own self-focused apprehensions and doubts. A famine, a flooded town, a serial killer on the loose, the resignation of a government, an economist's prediction of breadlines by next year; such outer turmoil is precisely what we might need in order to usher in a sense of inner calm.

Today the news informs us of a man who fell asleep at the wheel of his car after staying up late into the night committing adultery on the Internet – and drove off an overpass, killing a family of five in a caravan below. Another item speaks of a university student, beautiful and promising, who went missing after a party and was found in pieces in the trunk of a minicab five days later. A third rehearses the particulars of an affair between a tennis coach and her thirteen-year-old pupil. These occurrences, so obviously demented, invite us to feel sane and blessed by comparison. We can turn away from them and experience a new sense of relief at our predictable routines, at how tightly bound we have kept our more unusual desires and at our restraint in never yet having poisoned a colleague or entombed a relation under the patio.

5.

WHAT DOES ALL this news do to us over time? What remains of the months, even years we spend with it in aggregate? Whither those many excitements and fears: about the missing child, the budget shortfall and the unfaithful general? To what increase in wisdom did all these news stories contribute, beyond leaving behind a vague and unsurprising sediment of conclusions, for example, that China is rising, that central Africa is corrupt and that education must be reformed?

It is a sign of our mental generosity that we don't generally insist on such questions. We imagine that there would be something wrong in simply switching off. It is hard to give up on the habit first established in our earliest years, as we sat cross-legged during school assembly, of listening politely to figures of authority while they tell us about things they proclaim to be essential.

To ask why the news matters is not to presume that it doesn't, but to suggest the rewards of approaching our intake more self-consciously. This book is a record, a phenomenology, of a set of encounters with the news. It is framed around fragments of news culled from a variety of sources that have been subjected to analysis deliberately more elaborate than its creators intended, based on an assumption that these fragments might be no less worthy of study than lines of poetry or philosophy.

The definition of news has deliberately been left vague. Though there are obvious differences between news organizations, there are also enough similarities for it to seem possible to speak of a generic category that blurs into one the traditional fiefdoms of news – radio, TV, online and print – and the contrasting ideologies of right and left, high- and lowbrow.

This project has a utopian dimension to it. It not only asks what news currently is; it also tries to imagine what it could one day be. To dream of an ideal news organization shouldn't suggest an indifference to the current economic and social realities of the media;

rather it stems from a desire to break out of a range of pessimistic assumptions to which we may have become too easily resigned.

6.

MODERN SOCIETIES ARE still at the dawn of understanding what kind of news they need in order to flourish. For most of history, news was so hard to gather and expensive to deliver, its hold on our inner lives was inevitably kept in check. Now there is almost nowhere on the planet we are able to go to escape from it. It is there waiting for us in the early hours when we wake up from a disturbed sleep; it follows us on board planes making their way between continents; it is waiting to hijack our attention during the children's bedtime.

The hum and rush of the news have seeped into our deepest selves. What an achievement a moment of calm now is, what a minor miracle the ability to fall asleep or to talk undistracted with a friend – and what monastic discipline would be required to make us turn away from the maelstrom of news and listen for a day to nothing but the rain and our own thoughts.

We may need some help with what the news is doing to us: with the envy and the terror, with the excitement and the frustration; with all that we've been told and yet occasionally suspect we may be better off never having learned.

Hence a little manual that briefly tries to complicate a habit that, at present, has come to seem a bit too normal and harmless for our own good.

II.

Politics

Boredom & Confusion

TENANTS' RENT ARREARS SOAR IN PILOT
BENEFIT SCHEME ❡

ASSEMBLY ABORTION LAW CHANGE FAILS ❡

MIXED EFFORTS TO REBALANCE THE ECONOMY ❡

EUROPEAN COURT OF HUMAN RIGHTS
TO REACH IMMIGRATION JUDGEMENT ❡

COUNCIL SPENDING 'LACKING CLARITY' ❡

COMMITTEES MAKE GUN-RIGHTS
PROVISIONS PERMANENT ❡

ANTI-TAX GROUP LEADS CONSERVATIVE
CHARGE ❡

RECESS APPOINTMENTS RULING TO BE
APPEALED ❡

SYDNEY MAN CHARGED WITH CANNIBALISM
AND INCEST ❡

BBC

1.

IT IS EARLY morning and, still in bed, one reaches for a screen and navigates to the news. Soon it will be time for the shower and the usual rush to make it out of the house on schedule, but there are still a few moments left to browse.

Sadly, today nothing seems particularly tempting. The first, rather puzzling entry – 'Tenants' Rent Arrears Soar in Pilot Benefit Scheme' – gets a click anyway in the hope that something more intriguing may lie beyond it:

> Rent arrears among tenants on a government pilot project that pays housing benefit directly to recipients have seen a big increase, figures show. One area is predicting a £14m loss if the new system is implemented for all its tenants. Paying housing benefit directly to recipients, rather than their landlords, will form a key part of the planned new Universal Credit. The Department for Work and Pensions said the experiment has helped it to ensure that its scheme will be effectively implemented across the country. ❡

This is scarcely any better. A decision to change the way that the government subsidizes housing for the lowest-paid is clearly significant; a high-minded news organization has spent time and money bringing the particulars of the scheme to public attention. And yet it isn't easy to care.

This isn't unusual. We regularly come across headlines of apparent importance that, in private, leave us disengaged. Boredom and confusion may be two of the most common, but also two of the most shameful and therefore concealed, emotions provoked by so-called 'serious' political stories presented by the news organizations of modern democracies.

Further down the list of headlines, however, there is one story, about an incestuous cannibal in Australia, that requires no effort whatsoever.

Perhaps one is, at heart, a truly shallow and irresponsible citizen.

2.

BUT BEFORE CASTIGATING ourselves too strongly, imagine if, in similar circumstances, we had been shown a headline that read simply 'Man in Russia Consults Lawyer', beneath which lay the following story:

> Three women: an old lady, a young lady, and a trades-man's wife; and three gentlemen: one a German banker with a ring on his finger, another a bearded merchant, and the third an irate official in uniform with an order hanging from his neck, had evidently long been waiting. Two clerks sat at their tables writing, and the sound of their pens was audible. The writing-table accessories (of which Karenin was a connoisseur) were unusually good, as he could not help noticing. One of the clerks, without rising from his chair, screwed up his eyes and addressed Karenin ill-humouredly.

'What do you want?'
'I want to see a lawyer on business.' ¶

Imagine if at this point the story came to a sudden halt, and we were expected to express deep fascination and a desire to know more, even though it wasn't clear when 'more' would appear and it might be many weeks before a dozen further lines of this wearisome tale were made available.

It would be implausible to suppose that we could nurture a sincere interest in *Anna Karenina* in this way, but the habit of randomly dipping readers into a brief moment in a lengthy narrative, then rapidly pulling them out again, while failing to provide any explanation of the wider context in which events have been unfolding, is precisely what occurs in the telling of many of the most important stories that run through our societies, whether an election, a budget negotiation, a foreign policy initiative or a change to the state benefit system. No wonder we get bored.

3.

WE'RE STANDING FAR too close. To draw another analogy from the arts, it is as if we were being asked to open our eyes a millimetre or two above an inchoate bluish-purple surface marked with random black dashes tinged white along their edges. For all we could tell from such a vantage point, we might well be looking at the landscape of Jupiter, the surface of a bruise or the fossilized footprints of a prehistoric creature – none of them especially engaging options. Yet we might in fact be gazing at a detail of one of the most psychologically compelling portraits in Western art, Titian's *Portrait of Gerolamo Barbarigo*, only at the wrong distance – for this is a masterwork that requires a viewer to be standing at least a metre away from it before it begins to yield any of its interest.

4.

BOREDOM IS A new challenge and responsibility. For most of human history, there simply wasn't any news to be bored by. What information there was lay in the hands of a small and secretive aristocratic governing class. It went only to the few: the king, the chancellor, the commander of the army and the senior members of trading companies.

Now the news is for everyone, and yet the wheels of our curiosity are too often at risk of spinning idly in a soft slush of data. It is as if, every day before breakfast, a stern and alarmed civil servant rushed in to see us with a briefcase filled with a bewildering and then in the end tiring range of issues: 'Five hospitals are predicted to breach their credit limits by the end of the month', 'The central bank is worried about its ability to raise money on the bond markets', 'A Chinese warship has just left the mainland en route for Vietnam', 'The Canadian prime minister will be here for dinner tomorrow'.

What are we meant to think? Where should all this go in our minds?

Who cares?

Titian, *Portrait of Gerolamo Barbarigo*, c. 1510.

5.

NEWS ORGANIZATIONS ARE coy about admitting that what they present us with each day are minuscule extracts of narratives whose true shape and logic can generally only emerge from a perspective of months or even years – and that it would hence often be wiser to hear the story in chapters rather than snatched sentences. They are institutionally committed to implying that it is inevitably better to have a shaky and partial grasp of a subject this minute than to wait for a more secure and comprehensive understanding somewhere down the line.

Given the dangers of confusion that result, what we need above all are good signposts. Under a headline such as 'Man in Russia Consults Lawyer', an extract from a novel – even one of *Anna Karenina*'s power – will seem irksome. However, if we were told that we were reading a small, slightly monotonous passage that belonged to an extraordinary thousand-page book exploring the tragic dimensions of marriage, in particular the tension between the desire for adventure and the demands of domesticity and social conformity, we might anticipate a next instalment with a little more excitement.

We need news organizations to help our curiosity by signalling how their stories fit into the larger themes on which a sincere capacity for interest depends. To grow interested in any piece of information, we need somewhere to 'put' it, which means some way of connecting it to an issue we already know how to care about. A section of the human brain might be pictured as a library in which information is shelved under certain fundamental categories. Most of what we hear about day to day easily signals where in the stacks it should go and gets immediately and unconsciously filed: news of an affair is put on the heavily burdened shelf dedicated to How Relationships Work, a story of the sudden sacking of a CEO slots into our evolving understanding of Work & Status.

But the stranger or the smaller stories become, the harder the shelving process grows. What we colloquially call 'feeling bored' is just the mind, acting out of a self-preserving reflex, ejecting information it has despaired of knowing where to place. We might, for example, struggle to know what to do with information that a group of Chinese officials was paying a visit to Afghanistan to discuss border security in the province of Badakhshan or that a left-wing think tank was agitating to reduce levels of tax in the pharmaceutical industry. We might need help in transporting such orphaned pieces of information to the stacks that would most appropriately reveal their logic.

It is for news organizations to take on some of this librarian's work. It is for them to give us a sense of the larger headings under which minor incidents belong. An item on a case of petty vandalism one Saturday night in a provincial town ('Bus Shelter Graffitied by Young Vandals in Bedford') might come to life if it was viewed as a minuscule moment within a lengthier drama titled 'The Difficulties Faced by Liberal Secular Societies Trying to Instil Moral Behaviour without the Help of Religion'. Likewise, an indigestible item about yet another case of government corruption in the Democratic Republic of Congo ('Kickback Accusations in DRC') could be enhanced by a heading that hinted at its grander underlying subject: 'The Clash Between the Western Understanding of the State and the African Notion of the Clan'.

Properly signposted, even the unfortunate account of the change to the government housing benefit system would stand a chance. In reality, this article is no more about what its headline announces – 'Tenants' Rent Arrears Soar in Pilot Benefit Scheme' – than *Anna Karenina* is about a man in Russia who consults a lawyer. It is about the ongoing enquiry by the modern state into how best to assist its poorest members; it is part of a hundred-year debate about whether welfare lends its recipients dignity and support or subtly humiliates them by fostering dependence. It is a single episode in a multi-chaptered narrative that might be called 'How Subsidy Affects Character', 'The Psychology of Aid' or, more sonorously and abstractly, 'The Responsibility for Poverty'.

6.

UNFORTUNATELY FOR OUR levels of engagement, there is a prejudice at large within many news organizations that the most prestigious aspect of journalism is the dispassionate and neutral presentation of 'facts'. CNN's slogan, for instance, is 'Bringing you the facts'; NRC Handelsblad of the Netherlands touts its ability to 'deliver fact, not opinion'; the BBC vaunts itself as 'the world's most reliable source of facts'.

The problem with facts is that there is nowadays no shortage of sound examples. The issue is not that we need more of them, but that we don't know what to do with the ones we have. Every news day unleashes another flood: we learn that Standard & Poor's is reviewing the nation's credit rating, that there has been an extension to the government spending bill, that voting boundaries have been submitted to a committee and that plans for a natural-gas pipeline have begun to be drawn up. But what do these things actually *mean*? How are they related to the central questions of political life? What can they help us to understand?

The opposite of facts is *bias*. In serious journalistic quarters, bias has a very bad name. It is synonymous with malevolent agendas, lies and authoritarian attempts to deny audiences the freedom to make up their own minds.

Yet we should perhaps be more generous towards bias. In its pure form, a bias simply indicates a method of evaluating events that is guided by a coherent underlying thesis about human functioning and flourishing. It is a pair of lenses that slide over reality and aim to bring it more clearly into focus. Bias strives to explain what events mean and introduces a scale of values by which to judge ideas and events. It seems excessive to try to escape from bias per se; the task is rather to find ways to alight on its more reliable and fruitful examples.

Although certain grating right- and left-wing varieties dominate our understanding of the term bias, there are ultimately as many biases as there are visions of life. There are countless worthy lenses to slide between ourselves and the world. We might, for example, interpret the news according to the distinctive biased perspectives of Walt Whitman or Jane Austen, Charles Dickens or the Buddha. One could imagine a news outlet with a psychoanalytic bias, focusing on issues of guilt and envy on both sides of the Arab–Israeli conflict, alive to the idea of projection in political debates and highly sceptical that 'depression' had set in across the country because the economy had contracted by 0.1 per cent or indeed that happiness was inevitable because it was set to expand by 1.3 per cent.

What should be laudable in a news organization is not a simple capacity to collect facts, but a skill – honed by intelligent bias – at teasing out their relevance.

7.

CENTRAL TO MODERN politics is the majestic and beautiful idea that every citizen is – in a small but highly significant way – the ruler of his or her own nation. The news has a central role to play in the fulfilment of this promise, for it is the conduit through which we meet our leaders, judge their fitness to direct the state and evolve our positions on the most urgent economic and social challenges of the day. Far from being incidental features of democracies, news organizations are their guarantors.

And yet the news as it exists is woefully short on the work of coordination, distillation and curation. We are in danger of getting so distracted by the ever-changing agenda of the news that we wind up unable to develop political positions of any kind. We may lose track of which of the many outrages really matters to us and what it was that we felt we cared so passionately about only hours ago. At the very moment when our societies have reached a stage of unparalleled complexity, we have impatiently come to expect all substantial issues to be capable of drastic compression. Faced with the scale of the problems the news highlights, individual initiative can start to seem counter-intuitive and bathetic. Rather than an impression of political possibility, an encounter with the news may usher in an impression of our nothingness in an unimprovable and fundamentally chaotic universe.

8.

HEGEL'S ARGUMENT THAT the news now occupies the same prestigious position in society as religion once did misses out an important difference between the two fields of knowledge: religions have traditionally been particularly sensitive to how bad we are at focusing on anything. Exactly like the news, religions want to tell us important things every day. But unlike the news, they know that if they tell us too much, in one go, and only once, then we will remember – and do – *nothing*.

They therefore take care to serve up only a little of their fare each day, taking us patiently through a few issues and then returning to them again and again. Repetition and rehearsal are key to the pedagogical methods of the major faiths. They know there is no point informing us of a vital cause in a hurried and excitable way. They sit us down in a solemn place, quieten our minds and then speak to us with dignified urgency rather than panic, understanding that we will have to return to their ideas over days and weeks if we are to stand any chance of being influenced in how we think and behave.

9.

IT WOULD BE easy to suppose that the real enemy of democratic politics must be the active censorship of news – and therefore that the freedom to say or publish anything would be the natural ally of civilization.

But the modern world is teaching us that there are dynamics far more insidious and cynical still than censorship in draining people of political will; these involve *confusing*, *boring* and *distracting* the majority away from politics by presenting events in such a disorganized, fractured and intermittent way that a majority of the audience is unable to hold on to the thread of the most important issues for any length of time.

A contemporary dictator wishing to establish power would not need to do anything so obviously sinister as banning the news: he or she would only have to see to it that news organizations broadcast a flow of random-sounding bulletins, in great numbers but with little explanation of context, within an agenda that kept changing, without giving any sense of the ongoing relevance of an issue that had seemed pressing only a short while before, the whole interspersed with constant updates about the colourful antics of murderers and film stars. This would be quite enough to undermine most people's capacity to grasp political reality – as well as any resolve they might otherwise have summoned to alter it. The status quo could confidently remain forever undisturbed by a flood of, rather than a ban on, news.

A popular perception that political news is boring is no minor issue; for when news fails to harness the curiosity and attention of a mass audience through its presentational techniques, a society becomes dangerously unable to grapple with its own dilemmas and therefore to marshal the popular will to change and improve itself.

But the answer isn't just to intimidate people into consuming more 'serious' news; it is to push so-called serious outlets into learning to present important information in ways that can properly engage audiences. It is too easy to claim that serious things must be, and can almost afford to be, a bit boring. The challenge is to transcend the current dichotomy between those outlets that offer thoughtful but impotent instruction on the one hand and those that provide sensationalism stripped of responsibility on the other.

In the ideal news organization of the future, the ambitious tasks of contextualization and popularization would be taken so seriously that stories about welfare payments would be (almost) as exciting as those about incestuous Antipodean cannibals.

A Little Hope

Manchester city centre was torn apart by looters as young as nine in the worst riots in the city for 30 years. Hundreds of youths and 'feral' children stormed through the streets smashing windows and stealing clothing, mobile phones and jewellery. Shops and bins were set on fire as police struggled to keep up with marauding gangs in a cat-and-mouse chase across the city. Yesterday police chiefs admitted they had been 'overwhelmed' by the scale of the disturbances and had to call on neighbouring forces to assist. ❡

Daily Mail

1.

WHAT KIND OF country do we live in? What is the average person in it like? Should we feel scared or reassured, proud or ashamed?

The first thing to admit is that we can't answer these questions on the basis of our own experience alone. It is so hard to get to know a nation. Even the smallest countries have so many people in them that no individual could hope to meet up with more than a fraction of them across a highly sociable lifetime. Furthermore, there are not many large-scale public spaces where citizens can directly get acquainted. We don't often make new friends at the mall or get much of an insight into our fellow inhabitants at the cinema. Perhaps it used to be easier. In ancient Athens, for instance, thanks to good weather, a small and cohesive city centre and a culture of democratic conviviality (at least for some), there must have been regular opportunities to take the pulse of society as a whole at first hand. But we aren't so blessed. Our cities are too big, our weather patterns too unpredictable, our democratic systems too indirect and our homes too widely scattered.

We are therefore left to form impressions of our communities in indirect ways, in our imaginations rather than in actuality, and we do so with the help of two tools in particular.

2.

THE FIRST OF these is architecture. Through their appearance, a country's streets, houses, offices and parks combine to convey a psychological portrait of those who designed and inhabit them.

Contrasting visions of what 'other people' might be like.
Amsterdam docks (top), London docks (bottom).

If you were trying to understand the character of the modern Netherlands and were wandering Amsterdam's eastern docklands, you might conclude on the basis of the architecture alone that the Dutch were a forward-looking, playful, peaceable, family-centred people whom you might want to get to know better, and whose existence seemed a source of hope and reassurance.

Contrast this with the messages emanating from another city waterside redevelopment project, this one at Pier Parade in North Woolwich, London. Here the water-stained, derelict, cracking concrete buildings suggest that despair is to be expected and that the best way to resolve an argument would be to shout or shoot. Laughter and innocence feel unwelcome.

We don't, of course, always have to follow these architectural cues. We might be furious and downcast in Amsterdam's docks and full of vim and defiant energy in Pier Parade. It is just a little more unlikely.

3.

THE SECOND TOOL with which we get to know the character of others is, of course, the news. It is the news that introduces us to a far wider range of human beings than we could ever meet in person, and that over time, through the stories it runs and the way it comments on them, forms an idea in our minds about the kind of country we live in.

And so it is that, every day when we follow the news, we can count on learning some extremely dark truths about the people around us:

Mother accused of starving her four-year-old son to death ¶

Members of sex ring threatened to cut off the face of one of their victims and decapitate her baby after she tried to tell police ¶

Man kept his wife chained up in the basement and whipped her with dog chains ¶

Church-going woman, 51, used anti-freeze to kill husband she hated and son who was worse than a pest before poisoning daughter who would not get a job ¶

Factory worker sexually assaulted two 13-year-old girls while picking fruit ¶

Pilot bludgeoned wealthy wife to death because he felt humiliated ¶

Toddler bled to death in hospital due to 'catastrophic' lack of communication between doctors ¶

Man tried to chop off his ex-girlfriend's hands with a meat cleaver ¶

Daily Mail

4.

THESE STORIES HAVE more impact on us than we might presume. They are read every day by many millions. They are more interesting than most novels and some of our friends. Without our meaning for this to happen, they seep into our minds and colour our views of strangers. After reading such stories, many things become harder.

It becomes more difficult to be hopeful:
Britain facing triple economic calamity ¶

It feels riskier to order a taxi:
No woman is safe in a minicab, warns rape judge ¶

Or to take a train:
Homeless man found guilty of pushing 84-year-old woman
to her death on station platform ¶

One worries about getting ill:
'Most lethal ever' new flu virus kills third of victims ¶

But one worries even more about going to hospital:
Patient, 39, died after waiting eight hours without water and
an 'extraordinary lack of care' ¶

One longs to be young again:
Miley Cyrus wears racy tight white briefs and black thigh-high
boots for raunchy morning television performance ¶

But one loses all faith in innocence:
Teacher gives student, 16, pot and has sex with him more than
eight times ¶

One worries about the state of one's body:
Chloe Sevigny shows off her legs in printed shorts at the
Orange Is the New Black premiere ¶

And knows how people will judge us when we are older:
What has happened to Meg Ryan's face? ¶

One worries about birds:
Customers' horror as they find dead bird in bag of salad
during their meal ❡

And one worries about insects:
Woman finds live giant Egyptian grasshopper in her bag
of greens ❡

One hates politicians:
EU leaders quaffed £120 bottles of wine over lunch while insisting there was no room to make savings in the Brussels budget ❡

But one doesn't hold out much hope for ordinary people
either:
Wheelchair-bound equalities adviser, 59, jailed for arranging
to have sex with girl, five, and her mother at a Travelodge ❡

One is fearful of men:
Father murdered his 11-month-old son by shaking him violently
and throwing him on the floor minutes after argument with his
girlfriend ❡

But one is equally afraid of women:
Mother, 43, arrested for having an affair with her teenage
daughter's 14-year-old friend ❡

One realizes how provincial one's life is:
Kate Moss and Naomi Campbell party with Grace Jones
until 5am following star-studded gallery bash ❡

And how devoid of passion one's relationship has become:
Like the honeymoon never ended: Keira Knightley can't stop
cuddling husband ❡

There seem very few reasons not to despair of the human race: Suri Cruise, 7, to launch her own fashion range ¶

Daily Mail

5.

IF ASKED WHY it has decided to tell us all this, and is driving us more than a little mad as a result, the news will soberly reply that it has no choice. It simply has a duty to tell us 'the truth'. What happens in a country is not something that it *decides*. The stories aren't made up: a father really did murder his eleven-month-old son. A wheelchair-bound equalities adviser truly did arrange to have sex with a five-year-old girl and her mother at a Travelodge. It would be a betrayal of journalistic duty to keep the public away from these sobering but fundamental phenomena; journalists have to share the truth about the nation with the same frankness and lack of squeamishness as a doctor delivering a challenging diagnosis.

6.

YET THIS ISN'T entirely true. In any nation at any given point there is a welter of conflicting evidence about what is going on in the land. There will be several paedophiliac murderers at work, but there will also be tens of millions who don't favour abusing and bludgeoning children to death. Some people will be drawn to murdering partners who have been unfaithful with a meat cleaver, but the majority will tearfully and angrily muddle along. There will be some depressed residents who have been worn down by economic hardships, but they will have their opposites in many others who remain resilient in the face of daunting odds. Some people will riot and vomit in the streets, break shop windows and run off with looted spirits, but most will be keener to trim back the flowers in the garden and keep things tidy in the kitchen. A few people will go to glamorous parties all the time, but many more will accept with grace the pleasures, dignity and freedom of an ordinary life. It is easy to get upset about the deteriorating state of one's body, but there are other ways to excel and impress than via one's legs.

Strangely though, the more cheerful side of the coin never makes it into the news. There is a plethora of headlines that would be both true and yet impossible to run:

Grandmother, 87, helped three flights up the stairs at railway station by 15-year-old bystander she didn't know ¶

Teacher surmounts his feelings for a young student ¶

Man abandons rash plan to kill his wife after brief pause ¶

65 million people go to bed every night without murdering or hitting anyone ¶

There are so many different versions of 'reality', it is impossible to speak of the nation as if it were a single thing that could daily be captured by the most determined news organizations. The news may present itself as the authoritative portraitist of reality. It may claim to have an answer to the impossible question of what has really been going on, but it has no overarching ability to transcribe reality. It merely selectively *fashions* reality through the choices it makes about which stories to cast its spotlight on and which ones to leave out.

Herein rests an enormous and largely uncomprehended power: the power to assemble the picture that citizens end up having of one another; the power to dictate what our idea of 'other people' will be like; the power to invent a nation in our imaginations.

This power is so significant because the stories the news deploys end up having such a self-determining effect. If we are regularly told that many of our countrymen are crazed and violent, we will be filled with fear and distrust every time we go outside. If we receive subtle messages that money and status matter above all, we will feel humiliated by an ordinary life. If it's implied that all politicians lie, we'll quietly put our idealism and innocence aside and mock every one of their plans and pronouncements. And if we're told that the economy is the most important indicator of fulfilment and that it will be a disaster for a decade at least, we will be unable to face reality with much confidence ever again.

7.

BEFORE WE DESPAIR at the calamities that apparently surround us on all sides, we should remember that the news is ultimately only one set of stories about what is happening out there, no more and no less.

Our nation isn't just a severed hand, a mutilated grandmother, three dead girls in a basement, embarrassment for a minister, trillions of debt, a double suicide at the railway station and a fatal five-car crash by the coast.

It is also the cloud floating right now unattended over the church spire, the gentle thought in the doctor's mind as he approaches the patient's bare arm with a needle, the field mice by the hedgerow, the small child tapping the surface of a newly hard-boiled egg while her mother looks on lovingly, the nuclear submarine patrolling the maritime borders with efficiency and courage, the factory producing the first prototypes of a new kind of engine and the spouse who, despite extraordinary provocations and unkind words, discovers fresh reserves of patience and forgiveness.

This, too, is reality. The news we are given about the nation is not *the* nation.

8.

WHY DO NEWS organizations focus so much on the darkness? Why so much grimness and so little hope? Perhaps they think that their audiences are by nature a little too innocent, sheltered and pleased with themselves and therefore very much in need of being taught some of the negative aspects of reality – in order to recalibrate their expectations of others and take safety measures where possible. The presumption is that without the dark realism of the news, the nation might lapse back into its dangerous tendency to gloss over its problems and feel foolishly content with itself.

Putting aside the logic of this thesis for a moment, it at least offers up a suggestion of how news organizations should go about curating their content. Faced with an infinity of potential stories, they should pick ones that answer to what they think of as the prevailing national *need*. That which the nation most needs to hear at any given point – in order to compensate for its weaknesses – should determine the selection process behind the line-up of news items.

This logic isn't alien to news organizations of today. What is problematic is their judgement about what the national need actually is. Most countries, far from taking too rosy a view of their condition, far from trusting too much and feeling stupidly hopeful, do precisely the opposite. They are at risk for reasons other than the ones currently implicitly diagnosed by the media. They scupper their chances through excessive fear, anxiety and gloom. They are all too familiar with their litanies of problems, and yet they seem to feel debilitatingly small, unambitious and weak in the face of them. They can't see a way past decline, broken relationships, out-of-control teenagers, status anxiety, physical vulnerability and economic ruin.

There is a task for the news here: not only to remind us daily of society's worst failings, but also – sometimes – to train and direct its capacities for pride, resilience and hope. National decline can be precipitated not only or principally by sentimental optimism, but also by a version of media-induced clinical depression.

9.

ARCHITECTURE CAN OFFER a useful example of how the occasional showcasing of what is positive has legitimate uses. The members of the team charged with designing the velodrome for the 2012 London Olympics (less than a mile from North Woolwich) were well aware of Britain's many challenges – its class divisions and economic inequalities, its educational failures and its housing shortages, its high rates of family breakdown and its degraded manners and morals – but they decided, on this occasion, not to dwell on them.

Instead they chose to create a structure that would stand as an eloquent expression of politeness, modernity, class harmony and reconciliation with nature, in the hope that these qualities might become more present in the country at large through their articulation in a cycling venue clad in glass, steel and western red cedar. The building was an essay in flattery. It hinted that desirable qualities were already widely possessed by a country in which they were in fact only nascent or intermittent.

We are used to thinking of flattery as sentimental and dangerous, an abandonment of reality, but this is to underestimate how reality can be moulded. The child who is praised for her first modest attempts at kindness (when sharing a toy with a neighbour's offspring), and called lovely as a result, is being guided to develop beyond what she actually happens to be right now. The thought is that she will grow into the person she has flatteringly been described as already being.

As with architecture, so with news. Alongside its usual focus on catastrophe and evil, the news should perform the critical function of sometimes distilling and concentrating a little of the hope a nation requires to chart a course through its difficulties. While helping society by uncovering its misdeeds and being honest about its pains, the news should not neglect the equally important task of constructing an imaginary community that seems sufficiently good, forgiving and sane that one might want to contribute to it.

This is perhaps (also) what 'other people' might one day be like in Britain:
a suggestion from the Olympic Velodrome, London, 2012.

Fear & Anger

PANIC AS METEOR INJURES HUNDREDS ❡ **NBC**

ATYPICAL PNEUMONIA LIKELY
TO SPREAD ❡ *Sydney Morning Herald*

OFFICE CHAIRS COULD BE FATAL ❡ *Business Week*

EBOOKS ARE BAD FOR CHILDREN ❡ *Guardian*

POLITICAL FUTURE IN SHAMBLES ❡ **CNN**

INEXCUSABLE BUNGLING
IN PARLIAMENT ❡ *Daily Telegraph*

1.

TWO EMOTIONS WITH which we're likely to become extremely well acquainted the longer we spend with the news are fear and anger.

The news leaves us in no doubt that there are a lot of things in the world which we should be very scared about: extraterrestrial objects, mutating viruses, office furniture, technology … In relation to these and many other ills, the news directs us to adopt a distinctive stance: one of timidity, panic and fragility. Our chances of surviving the difficulties facing humanity are deemed to be very slim – though slightly increased if we habitually keep up with the headlines.

2.

IN ITS STOKING of our fears, the news cruelly exploits our weak hold on a sense of perspective.

In the visual arts, having perspective means a capacity to see different things in their true spatial relations: what is far away looks distant and smaller, what is near looks closer and larger. It was surprisingly difficult for artists to learn how to achieve perspective on a canvas – which suggests that the manoeuvre may be equally challenging in other areas of our lives.

Applied to the news, having perspective involves an ability to compare an apparently traumatic event in the present with the experiences of humanity across the whole of its history – in order to work out what level of attention and fear it should fairly demand.

With perspective in mind, we soon realize that – contrary to what the news suggests – hardly anything is totally novel, few

Village evacuated as severe floods hit swathes of Britain

Wallington, in Hampshire, was one of many parts of Britain that were inundated, leaving motorists stranded on roads, cars submerged and even resulting in a caravan being washed away. ¶

Daily Telegraph

things are truly amazing and very little is absolutely terrible. The revolution will not mean the end of history; it will just change a lot of things in many different small and complicated ways. The economic indices are grim, but we have weathered comparable drops many times over the last century and even the worst scenarios only predict that we will return to a standard of living we had a few decades ago, when life was still possible. A bad avian flu may disrupt international travel and defeat known drugs for a while, but research laboratories will eventually understand and contain it. The floods look dramatic, but in the end they will affect merely a fraction of the population and recede soon enough. Cancers and heart attacks have multiple causes that we may never understand completely, but eternal life was never on the agenda. Rome fell, but 600 years later everything was almost back to normal again.

Our capacity for calm ultimately depends on our levels of expectation: if we suppose that most things normally turn out to be slightly disappointing (but that this is OK); that change occurs slowly (but that life is long); that most people are neither terribly good nor very wicked (and this includes us); that humanity has faced crisis after crisis (yet muddled through) – if we are able to keep these entirely obvious but highly fugitive thoughts alive in our minds, then we stand to be less easily seduced into panic.

But we shouldn't be surprised if this kind of stoicism is of no interest whatsoever to the news, for it has sound commercial incentives for overemphasizing our vulnerability. Naturally the news badly needs its audience to feel agitated, frightened and bothered a lot of the time – yet we have an even greater responsibility to try to remain resilient.

3.

WHEN NEWS ISN'T frightening us, it is often busy enraging us. The ability to post comments at the end of online news stories has revealed a hitherto unimaginable level of anger in the population at large. To judge from the comments, it would seem that most of us are completely furious most of the time:

EU struggles to reach budget agreement

COMMENTS

Concerned Citizen 2 HOURS AGO
When oh when will we step off this treadmill!!!!!!!!!!

Chaffinch 2 HOURS AGO
There is a crisis here, but the trouble is that the politicians cannot fix it. Why? Because the basic concept on which the European Union was formed is flawed – and it can never work as it is. We need a two-tier system. Why didn't they solve this problem first – and only then get round to a realistic budget?!

Muishkin 4 MINUTES AGO
This comment was removed because the moderators found it broke the house rules about language. ¶

BBC

Beneath the rage, one senses a touching belief that the problems of the world are basically solvable, it's just they aren't being dealt with swiftly or decisively enough for the simple reason, to which every new day provides fresh testimony, that *we are ruled by crooks and idiots.* The relevant insights are there, just in the wrong hands. Herein lies a central paradox of the news: it gives us the tools to develop views on serious and consequential decisions which have a direct impact on our lives. It invites us to the conference table and into the parliament, it introduces us to the key players, then it shows us nothing but inexplicable delays, strange compromises and maddening evasions. It can feel as though we are daily being invited to watch helplessly while a close friend drowns behind a plate-glass window.

The news routinely tantalizes us with the promise of drastic change and improvement. It anoints certain politicians as visionaries and expresses confidence that they can fundamentally transform the nation within a few months of attaining office. It breathlessly awaits the arrival of the new head of the central bank, who might liberate the slumbering energies of capitalism. It takes us to conferences and encourages us to believe that the delegates might in three days of horsetrading solve some of the major issues of the globe, relating to economics, African poverty or the warming of the atmosphere.

Then everything falls apart. The politician turns out to be a fool and is dismissed as shallow and complacent, the central bank governor cites the behaviour of the bond market as the reason for renewed caution, the conferences get bogged down in petty squabbling and one or two of the delegates are even discovered to have cheated on their hotel bills.

If we're tempted to leave comments with unpublishably foul language in them at the end of stories, it may be because the news is reluctant ever to provide us with a sufficiently rich set of descriptions of the problems that surround issues. The most logical solutions regularly look as if they were being ignored *out of sheer stupidity*. We ask with impatience and eventual fury, 'Why don't they just…?' Without going too far in the direction of fatalism and trusting obedience, this righteous question should at once make us suspicious. It should be a cue for a range of serious answers, rather than remaining merely a rhetorical enquiry. What the news seldom bothers to mention is *why* things don't change very much; *why* great power and resources can't solve our difficulties at a stroke. It doesn't induct us with any degree of subtlety into the genuine reasons for calling a decision 'difficult'. It leaves us instead to assume with mounting fury that every ongoing problem can only be the result of intense laziness, stupidity or malevolence – and could be solved in a few relatively decisive and simple steps by someone intelligent and ingenious (perhaps the journalist herself).

Our rage would in large measure be appeased if we were made aware of the raft of complications slightly offstage which none of the parties have sought to draw attention to; if we were reminded that a so-called solution may set off a secondary wave of problems; if we were made to feel the pressures around the table and the miserably tough choices on the agenda and (in some cases at least) the essential goodwill of many of the participants; if we were richly inducted into why difficult decisions *are* difficult.

4.

THOUGH ANGER SEEMS a pessimistic response to a situation, it is at root a symptom of hope: the hope that the world can be better than it is. The man who shouts every time he loses his house keys is betraying a beautiful but rash faith in a universe in which keys never go astray. The woman who grows furious every time a politician breaks an election promise reveals a precariously utopian belief that elections do not involve deceit.

The news shouldn't eliminate angry responses; but it should help us to be angry for the right reasons, to the right degree, for the right length of time – and as part of a constructive project.

And wherever this isn't possible, then the news should help us with mourning the twisted nature of man and reconciling us to the difficulty of being able to imagine perfection while still not managing to secure it – for a range of stupid but nevertheless unbudgeable reasons.

The news currently resists giving us the single most calming response one can offer to certain problems: evidence that they are normal and that they belong to a species which is intrinsically (rather than exceptionally) imperfect. In hock to the excitements and commercial advantages of rage, the news cruelly ignores the project of consolation.

The most significant fact of political life, which almost no news organization will dare to acknowledge – because it would at a stroke exclude half of its speculations and disappointments – is that in some key areas of politics, *nothing can be achieved very quickly by any one person or party*; it would be impossible for *anyone* – not simply this fool or that group of cretins – to change matters at a pace that would flatter the expectations of the news cycle; and that in the case of certain problems, the only so-called 'solutions' will have to await a hundred years or more of incremental change, rather than a messianic leader, an international conference or a quick war.

5.

IN ITS THWARTED optimism, the news is the disillusioned progeny of the Enlightenment. Refusing to square with human nature, it allows our hopes to smash constantly against the same shoals; it greets every new day with faux cherubic innocence, only to stoke up rage and disillusionment at our condition by nightfall. It posits the potential existence of a perfect world which is forever almost within reach but then curiously slips out of grasp at every step of the political process. It doesn't do us the favour of conceding that in many respects we are a fundamentally – rather than incidentally – incorrigible species and that we would at key moments be wise to forgo hysterical annoyance for deep and quiet melancholy.

Baddies & the Bad

The Member of Parliament Eric Illsley is facing jail after pleading guilty to dishonestly claiming more than £14,000 in expenses. The claims were made for council tax, telephone usage, service charges and maintenance, and insurance and repairs at his second home in Renfrew Road, Kennington, south London. ¶

Daily Telegraph

1.

SOME OF JOURNALISM'S greatest triumphs have been connected
with exposés of powerful figures, on a fair number of occasions trig-
gering their subjects' downfall and even their incarceration.

The idea that words and pictures alone might prompt a resignation or a custodial sentence is a heady one for journalists, many
of whom continue to regard the Watergate investigation as the
central inspiration and beacon for their work.

When journalists are asked to explain what their most important contribution to society is, they will tend to emphasize one
function over any other: they will say that it is their responsibility
to hold 'power to account'.

2.

JOURNALISTS WOULD ARGUE that the powerful must be held to
account because they have strong tendencies to break the laws of
the land and to imagine themselves immune from prosecution:
they steal money, hide untaxed income, bribe their way around
legislation, contravene employment and environmental rules and
intimidate and sexually abuse the powerless.

Journalism is, according to this argument, primarily a branch
of the police force, as well as a proxy for the tax office and various
consumer groups. It first uncovers and then helps to prosecute
examples of law breaking and infraction which would have otherwise escaped attention, and so protects the interests of the ordinary,
voiceless citizen.

A world made safer: the British politician Eric Illsley heads to prison
for a year after a newspaper investigation into his expenses claims.
This is the Watergate paradigm in action.

3.

THE CLIMACTIC MOMENT when a powerful person is arrested at home after a news investigation can make for a mesmerizing spectacle. The police, acting in concert with news organizations, show up early; pictures are taken of the wrongdoer in his or her pyjamas, surprised in the act of eating toast or cereal. Sometimes a spouse or a child can be seen, crying, in the background.

Having the chance to bear vicarious witness to such an incident can provide appeasement for a range of emotions, including a sense of injustice, feelings of humiliation and a basic sense that the world must henceforth never again be left in the hands of incompetents and crooks.

In showing us the criminal about to be hauled off in the back seat of a police car, the news offers us the hope that the representative source of a myriad of our and our society's ills has now been identified and safely neutralized.

4.

THOUGH MANY POWERFUL people are routinely and very usefully brought to book by the news, many of the most significant difficulties of developed nations do not stem so neatly from the actions of baddies. An honest audit of these nations' greatest challenges reveals dilemmas and predicaments that include, but also range far beyond, criminal or contractual fraud at the top.

For example, it is often painfully hard to find an affordable and tolerably attractive neighbourhood to live in, but this doesn't seem to be the 'fault' of anyone who could be sent to prison. Far too many jobs pay too little, lack interest and status and are overseen by unpleasant managers and bosses, but it would be hard to know how to frame such problems in the language of a news scandal. A lot of commercial products seem unnecessary, garish, wasteful of resources and insultingly advertised – but here, too, nameable villains are hard to locate and charge.

The arrest of a crooked figure can beget a period of deep satisfaction, but the hopes it inspires may be misleading. Even if every last rotten plutocrat or powerful minister were locked up, nations would still have a thought-provoking number of problems to grapple with. We are likely to miss a great many matters of importance if we continue only to look for baddies of the kind a Watergate-style of journalism knows how to identify. We will fail to delve into many of the more systemic, impersonal but no less poisonous kinds of wrong that stand in relation to law breaking as passive aggression does to domestic violence: behaviours and values that are life-destroying and dispiriting but leave no outward marks and slip through the legal nets.

As currently structured, the news does not 'see' the property developer who condemns thousands of people to live in humiliating environments but who nevertheless breaks no laws and steals no money. The most assiduous reporter concerned with fraud won't be able to put a finger on anyone criminally responsible for the commercial messages that subtly erode the dignity and intelligence of public life or find anyone who can be arrested for a decline in politeness or respect between the sexes.

Properly conceived, investigative journalism should start with an all-encompassing interest in the full range of factors that sabotage group and individual existence. It would, among other things, investigate mental health, architecture, leisure time, family structures, relationships, the management styles of businesses, the educational curriculum and the status system – for these areas impact on our lives no less than events in the legislature.

The news may encourage us to imagine that the roots of a nation's problems have their fundamental origins in criminality at the top and yet, though there is clearly a role for targeting individual rotten apples, there is an equally vital task in directing attention to the colourless yet far larger institutional failures that lie concealed within our political and social arrangements.

5.

HOWEVER, THE SHEER intellectual difficulty of identifying the ills of society, together with an almost artistic longing to find a few individuals to whose names one can tidily pin the evils of life, can give rise to that well-known escapist alternative to true investigation: gaffe journalism.

A journalistic gaffe is something a powerful person inadvertently says or does in a momentary lapse which (as everyone knows) in no way reflects their considered views and yet which the news seizes upon and refuses to let go of, insisting that the gaffe must be an indicator of a deep and shameful truth.

Behind gaffe journalism lies the impotent rage of journalists who know that many things are deeply amiss in their country but who lack the access to power or the patience with bureaucracy that would enable them to pinpoint the true problems with any measure of accuracy.

The gaffe is prosecuted not because anyone sincerely believes that its exposure will subsequently lead to better policies or finer government. The gaffe merely provides an occasion for vengeance by a set of beleaguered individuals who have run out of ideas about how else to make a change.

6.

WHAT SHOULD THE news do with the bad guys? Currently, it passes on the worst of them to the police. But the majority it deals with through journalism's own distinctive instrument: humiliation. It shows reliable levels of enthusiasm for sarcastic stories, doorstep interviews, secret photographs and leaked correspondence. Flawed types must be turned *into* news and will then face the disgust of the moral-minded majority. The implicit idea is that society will be reformed through reputational ruin and public opprobrium.

But is shame really the most useful tool to be employed in the reformation of mankind? Do people grow better through being belittled? Does fear educate?

Too many of the stories about the misdeeds of bad people seem strikingly devoid of interest in the one goal that should rightly underpin all reports of wrongdoing and chicanery: *the ambition to help the nation to flourish.* These stories circle their fallen prey without any interest in the evolution of public life: they aren't trying to get accountancy, marriages, universities, immigration or the tax system to go better. They are just inviting us to have a particular kind of fun.

7.

JOURNALISM HAS BEEN too modest and too mean in defining its purpose merely as the monitoring of certain kinds of power; a definition that has harmfully restricted its conception of itself and its role in society. It is not just a de facto branch of the police or the tax office; it is, or should be, a government in exile that works through all issues of national life with a view to suggesting ways to build a better country.

The only honest purpose of unearthing and publicizing error is to make it less prevalent. Faced with corruption, idiocy and mediocrity, rather than remaining stuck at the level of gleeful fault finding in the present, the news should seek instead always to nurture greater competence in the future. However satisfying and important it can be to bring down the powerful, journalistic investigation should start with a subtly different and not invariably overlapping goal: the desire to try to improve things.

Received Ideas

The relentless march of three-dimensional printing continues ... [The process] uses exotic 'inks' based on silver and carbon nanotubes ... Carbomorph, because of its polyester component which melts when heated, is a suitable raw material for this process. It is also a useful one, for among its electrical properties is piezoresistivity. ¶

The Economist

1.

THE NOBLEST PROMISE of the news is that it will be able to alleviate ignorance, overcome prejudice and raise the intelligence of individuals and nations.

2.

BUT FROM SOME quarters it has intermittently been accused of a contrary capacity, that of making us completely stupid. One of the most uncompromising versions of this charge was levelled in the mid-nineteenth century by Gustave Flaubert. Flaubert belonged to a generation that had experienced the rise of mass-circulation newspapers at first hand. Whereas in his childhood news had been dispersed randomly throughout the population by rumour and via badly printed single-page news-sheets, by the time he was in his thirties the invention of the steam printing press, the development of railways and the relaxation of censorship laws had together enabled the proliferation of well-capitalized, authoritative newspapers which now laid claim, across France, to a combined readership of millions.

Flaubert was appalled by what, in his estimation, these newspapers were doing to the intelligence and curiosity of his countrymen. He believed that the papers were spreading a new kind of stupidity – which he termed '*la bêtise*' – into every corner of France, an idiocy that was far worse than the mere ignorance it replaced, for it was actively fuelled by, rather than just passively filling in for, knowledge. So contaminating was the effect of the press, in Flaubert's eyes, that only entirely illiterate and uneducated

Frenchmen now stood a chance of being able to think properly: 'Peasants are less idiotic than three-quarters of the middle classes of France, who are always getting themselves into a frenzy over something they've read in the papers and spinning like weather vanes according to whatever one paper or another is saying.'

The most loathsome character in *Madame Bovary*, the pharmacist Homais, is introduced early on as an avid consumer of news who sets aside a special hour every day to study '*le journal*' (Flaubert keeps the word in italics throughout, to send up the neo-religious reverence in which this object is held). In the evenings, Homais heads for an inn, Le Lion d'Or, where the local bourgeoisie gather to chew over current events: 'Afterwards, they discussed what was in "*the newspaper*". By this hour, Homais knew it all practically by heart, and he would report on it in full, including the editorials as well as the many individual catastrophes that had occurred across France and around the world.'

3.

FLAUBERT HATED NEWSPAPERS because of his conviction that they slyly encouraged readers to hand over to others a task that no honest person should ever consent to offload on to someone else: thinking. The press implicitly suggested that the formation of complex and intelligent opinions on important matters could now safely be entrusted to its employees, that the reader's mind could leave off its own particular peregrinations, enquiries and meditations and surrender wholesale to conclusions deftly packaged up by the leader writers of *Le Figaro* and its ilk.

It is hardly surprising that a writer so sensitive to cliché and the mentality of the herd should feel outraged by the constriction of independent enquiry that this mass development represented, by the ironing out of local eccentricity and individual difference in favour of an all-encompassing, monocultural set of assumptions. Here was a homogenizing force in danger of stamping out all the productive oddities of interior life and of turning the rich, idiosyncratic, handcrafted kitchen gardens of the mind into rolling, mechanized, insipid wheatfields.

4.

IN THE 1870S, Flaubert began keeping a record of what he judged to be the most idiotic patterns of thought promoted by the modern world in general and by the newspapers in particular. Published posthumously as *The Dictionary of Received Ideas*, this collection of bromides, organized by topic, was described by its author as an '*encyclopédie de la bêtise humaine*' (an encyclopedia of human stupidity). Here is a random sampling of its entries:

BUDGET Never balanced.
CATHOLICISM Has had a very good influence on art.
CHRISTIANITY Freed the slaves.
CRUSADES Benefited Venetian trade.
DIAMONDS To think that they're nothing but coal; if we came across one in its natural state, we wouldn't even bother to pick it up off the ground!

EXERCISE Prevents all illnesses. To be recommended
at all times.
PHOTOGRAPHY Will make painting obsolete.

It is worth noting how many of the *Dictionary*'s clichés touch
on sophisticated disciplines such as theology, science and politics,
without, however, going anywhere very clever with them: the
'received ideas' consist of exotic or intricate facts married to a stubborn narrowness of mind. In the past, Flaubert implied, idiots had
had no clue as to what the carbon structure of diamonds was. Their
shallowness had been entirely and reliably evident. But now the
press had made it very possible for a person to be at once unimaginative, uncreative, mean-minded *and* extremely well informed. The
modern idiot could routinely know what only geniuses had known
in the past, and yet he was still an idiot – a depressing combination
of traits that previous ages had never had to worry about. The news
had, for Flaubert, armed stupidity and given authority to fools.

5.

THE NEWS ORGANIZATIONS of our own day would be unlikely to
mollify Flaubert in the least. They continue to hammer their audiences' opinions into some highly standardized shapes:

3D PRINTING In future, everything will be 3D-printed.
Express surprise and awe at the prospect.
INTERNET Has made concentration impossible. So hard
now to read long novels.

WORK–LIFE BALANCE   More difficult than ever before.
It may soon be necessary to make an appointment to
see one's own spouse.

CARBON-FIBRE AIRCRAFT WINGS   Flex amazingly; but sure
to cause a crash one day.

MANDARIN   The language of the future.

6.

HOW DOES THE news manage to enlist us in its sometimes hack-
neyed or wrong-headed conclusions?

Primarily because it succeeds, by a variety of means, in coming across to us as extremely authoritative. For a start, we don't
entirely grasp who decides on what counts as news and by what
criteria – and therefore bulletins have a habit of seeming as if they
had been generated by nature or some higher necessity to which
we are not privy and which it would be impudent to question. We
forget the highly contingent and human dynamics underlying the
choice of what ends up being picked as a 'story'.

A certain coy secrecy is maintained about how news is even
made. We hear little, for example, about the three hours that the
political correspondent had to spend standing in the rain, posted
behind a barrier at the entrance to the Justus Lipsius building
in Brussels, just to record the prime minister's intemperate one-
line statement that he had nothing further to add to his original
press release of the day before; or about the hair-raising twenty-
two hours it took for the North African correspondent to catch
up with a group of rebels in Mali so that we might have a story

to skim over distractedly while eating a lunchtime sandwich; or about the travails of the photographer who lost too many hours of his life waiting for an actress to emerge from a coffee shop in Beverly Hills, to give us the pleasure of admiring a surprising new trench coat.

We are not supposed to think about, or even to be aware of, the serried ranks of giant black computer servers lined up for half a kilometre in data centres in Colorado or northern Finland, fuelled by dirty coal and natural gas: theirs is a dark physical reality unalluded to by our lightweight and luminous screens.

Though they radiate a cocksure impersonal importance beneath their headlines, the stories we take in were decided not by supernatural decree after a conclave of angels but by a group of usually rather weary and pressured editors struggling to assemble a plausible list of items in harried meetings in corner offices over muffins and coffee. Their headlines don't constitute an ultimate account of reality so much as some first hunches as to what might matter by mortals prey to the same prejudices, errors and frailties as the rest of us, hunches plucked out of a pool of several billion potential events that daily befall our species.

Whether a war in Africa should take priority over the launch of a shoe collection, a runaway tiger over a set of inflation figures, the rape of a pretty, white, middle-class schoolgirl over the decapitation of a homeless black man, the collapse of shares in mining companies over the first words spoken by a child depends on methods of classification that hint at society's most peculiar and clandestine prejudices.

We should at least be somewhat suspicious of the way that news sources, which otherwise expend considerable energy advertising their originality and independence of mind, seem so often to be in complete agreement on the momentous question of what happened today.

7.

INDIVIDUAL NEWS STORIES achieve power, too, by being delivered under the aegis of brands. Opinions that we might have probed more robustly had they been put to us by a person across a table can acquire an almost mythological power once they appear beneath certain mastheads.

We are marginally – but crucially – less likely to question the soundness of an article about a rationale for going to war when it comes presented beneath the neo-Gothic Cheltenham typeface of the *New York Times*, or to probe the coherence of a thesis defending a presidential budget when it is laid out in the sober yet sensuous columns of *Le Monde*'s Fenway font.

Brands alone dissuade us from picking sceptically at their underlying content.

8.

FOR ALL THE supposed plurality of the news, across outlets, the questions that end up being asked in a number of areas fail to range beyond some punishingly narrow boundaries.

In the field of education, it seems 'normal' to run stories about class sizes, teachers' pay, the country's performance in international league tables and the right balance between the roles of the private and state sectors. But we would risk seeming distinctly odd, even demented, if we asked whether the curriculum actually made sense; whether it really equipped students with the emotional and psychological resources that are central to the pursuit of good lives.

When it comes to housing, the news urges us to worry about how to get construction companies working, how to make purchasing a home easier for first-time buyers and how to balance the claims of nature against those of jobs and businesses. But it doesn't tend to find time to ask primordial, eccentric-sounding questions like: 'Why are our cities so ugly?'

In discussions of economics, our energy is channelled towards pondering what the right level of taxation should be and how best to combat inflation. But we are discouraged by mainstream news from posing the more peculiar, outlying questions about the ends of labour, the nature of justice and the proper role of markets.

News stories tend to frame issues in such a way as to reduce our will or even capacity to imagine them in profoundly other ways. Through its intimidating power, news numbs. Without anyone particularly rooting for this outcome, more tentative but potentially important private thoughts get crushed.

9.

MONEY IS PARTLY to blame. The financial needs of news companies mean that they cannot afford to advance ideas which wouldn't very quickly be able to find favour with enormous numbers of people. An artist can make a decent living selling work to fifty clients; an author can get by with 50,000 readers, but a news organization cannot pay its bills without a following larger than the population of a good-sized metropolis. What levels of agreement, what suppression of idiosyncrasy and useful weirdness, will be required to render material sufficiently palatable to so many … Wisdom, intelligence and subtlety of opinion tend not to be sprinkled through the population in handy blocks of 20 million people.

10.

ON ACCOUNT OF its scale and complexity, the world will always outstrip the capacity of any single body to ask fertile questions of it. News organizations will only ever be able to offer up sketchy and sometimes deeply mistaken maps of what will continue to be an infinitely elusive and varied reality.

Alarm bells should hence ring in our minds, as they rang in Flaubert's, upon any encounter with a point of view which seems to have attained a slightly too consistent level of consensus. We should remain at all times sceptically alert to the potentially gross idiocy that may lie concealed beneath the most beautiful fonts and the most authoritative and credible headlines. We should be as alert to media clichés as Flaubert was to literary ones. The latter ruin novels; the former can ruin nations.

III.

World News

Information/Imagination

The east of the Democratic Republic of Congo faces a catastrophic humanitarian crisis, an aid agency has warned ahead
of a regional summit in Uganda. The Oxfam charity said
millions of people were now at the mercy of militias, with a
sharp increase in killings, rapes and looting. It said the focus
on dealing with rebels had diverted the security forces from
other vulnerable areas. The UN says the conflict has forced
about 250,000 people from their homes. ⁋

BBC

I.

NEWS ORGANIZATIONS CAN be unexpectedly idealistic places. At the entrance to the headquarters of the BBC in London, there's a quotation in Latin on the wall which declares:

> This Temple of the Arts and Muses is dedicated to Almighty God by the first Governors of Broadcasting in the year 1931 ... It is their prayer that ... all things hostile to peace or purity may be banished from this house, and that the people, inclining their ear to what-soever things are beautiful and honest and of good report, may tread the path of wisdom and uprightness.

Upstairs the visitor can see how some of that idealism is translated into practical action. There are desks tasked with covering events in all the most troubled and unfortunate parts of the world. The staff concerned with Africa occupies an entire floor; Somalia alone has eight people reporting on it; the Democratic Republic of Congo has a cohort of three, who enjoy a sofa area and inspiring views on to Portland Place.

The idealistic line on news runs as follows: evil, passivity and racism are chiefly the results of ignorance. By helping people to learn what is really happening in other parts of the world, the chances of prejudice, fear, deceit and aggression decrease. News can make the world a better place.

2.

YET THERE IS a problem with this logic and it crops up on examination of the daily Web traffic figures for the BBC news website:

> Duchess of Cambridge Due to Give Birth in July 5.82M
> Heavier Snow Predicted across the UK 4.34M
> Bowie Comeback Makes Top 10 Singles Chart 2.52M
> Nigeria Church Attack in Kogi State Kills 19 9,920
> East DR Congo Faces Catastrophic
>   Humanitarian Crisis 4,450
> South Africa: Five Die in KwaZulu-Natal
>   'Clan Shooting' 2,540
> DR Congo Conflict: Kagame and Kabila
>   Fail to Agree 1,890

In one sense, the great goal of the Enlightenment has been achieved: the average citizen now has near-instantaneous access to information about events in every nation on earth. But we've also been forced to learn something rather more surprising: *no one is particularly interested.*

3.

THE STANDARD RESPONSE from news organizations is to blame the public for its shallowness, for caring more (by an astonishing margin) about a pop song than about a clan shooting, about the birth of one baby to a member of the British royal family than about 100,000 desperate children suffering from rickets and malaria in central Africa.

Yet what if this astonishing level of disengagement turned out to be not entirely the fault of the audience? What if the *real* reason viewers and readers don't much care about what is happening in foreign lands is not that we are especially shallow or nasty, nor even that the events described are inherently boring, but instead simply that *the news isn't being presented to us in a compelling* enough *way*? What if we have become uninterested in the world mainly because of certain mistaken assumptions the news organizations have made about the way the world should be *described* to us?

4.

THE FIRST OF these assumptions is that the single most important technical skill for every journalist to possess is the capacity to collect information accurately. Because news organizations presume that they are essentially battling the ignorance of their audiences, the gathering of precise information has a pride of place in the educational priorities of journalism schools. New entrants into the field are taught to seek out and transcribe quotations from key actors in each story, to provide facts and figures to back up any claims, to abstain from distractingly ornate writing and to strive to eliminate all personal and cultural bias from their reporting.

All of these strategies seem logical enough, but the problem is that the condition actually afflicting audiences differs slightly from the one diagnosed by the news establishment: they are in truth suffering not so much from *ignorance* as from *indifference*.

Accurate information about foreign countries is now not very hard to get hold of; the real issue is how we might come to feel sincere interest in any of it. It is one thing for a story to convey how many people died in an attack by guerrillas or were drowned in a flood or lost everything they owned because of a crooked president; in such coverage, the challenges are technical and administrative, the reporter needing to possess patience, bravery and an appetite for hard work. But it is another task altogether (one far less often considered) to persuade readers or viewers to *care* about such events. And the skills this requires lie in an area almost always overlooked by the foreign desks of news organizations.

Art may be most usefully defined as the discipline devoted to trying to get concepts powerfully into people's heads. In literature as distinct from journalism, the ablest practitioners will never assume that the bare bones of a story can be enough to win over their audience. They will not suppose that an attack or a flood or a theft must in and of itself carry some intrinsic degree of interest which will cause the reader to be appropriately moved or outraged. These writers know that no event, however shocking, can ever guarantee involvement; for this latter prize, they must work harder, practising their distinctive craft, which means paying attention to language, alighting on animating details and keeping a tight rein on pace and structure. In certain situations, creative writers may even choose to sacrifice strict accuracy – perhaps by adapting a fact, eliminating a point, compressing a quote or changing a date – and rather than feel that they are thereby carrying out a criminal act (the routine presumption of news organizations when they catch one of their own doing such things), they will instead understand that falsifications may occasionally need to be committed in the service of a goal higher still than accuracy: the hope of getting important ideas and images across to their impatient and distracted audiences.

5.

A SECOND ASSUMPTION guiding the reporting of foreign news holds that the more gruesome, tragic or macabre an incident is, the more 'important' it should be considered, and therefore the further up in the story hierarchy it should go. Journalists and their editors tend to believe that the importance of any event is determined by how anomalous and unusual it is, which almost invariably means how terrible, bloody and murderous it has proved to be. Therefore, a bombing that kills thirty people is thought more newsworthy than a quiet day in a fishing village, an outbreak of a tropical disease that tears its victims' lungs apart in three hours is considered to be of greater interest than the peaceful collection of the harvest, and revelations of torture by the security services are deemed more significant than a collective lunchtime ritual of eating tabbouleh and stuffed vine leaves in a bucolic field overlooking the River Jordan.

The problem with this philosophy is that unless we have some sense of what passes for normality in a given location, we may find it very hard to calibrate or care about *ab*normal conditions. We can be properly concerned about the sad and violent interruptions only if we know enough about the underlying steady state of a place, about the daily life, routines and modest hopes of its population.

Yet, when it comes to most other countries of the world, despite the news media's amazing technological capabilities, despite the bureaux, correspondents, photographers and camera operators, we are given no information whatsoever about ordinary occurrences. We don't know whether anyone has ever had a normal day in the Democratic Republic of Congo, for no such thing has ever been recorded by a Western news organization. We have no idea what it's like to go to school or visit the hairdresser in Bolivia; it's entirely mysterious whether anything like a good marriage is possible in Somalia; and we are equally in the dark about office life in Turkmenistan and what people do on the weekend in Algeria. The news parachutes us in only for the so-called 'important' events – the earthquakes, the gang rapes, the indiscriminate destruction of whole villages by drug-addled killers – and assumes that we will feel suitably shocked and drawn in by them.

But in truth, we can't much care about dreadful incidents unless we've first been introduced to behaviours and attitudes with which we can identify; until we have been acquainted with the sorts of mundane moments and details that belong to all of humanity. A focus on these does not in any way distract from 'serious' news; it instead provides the bedrock upon which all sincere interest in appalling and disruptive events must rest.

Critics of this argument might point out that we don't need to see or read stories about regular life in our own country before we can start caring about the irregular events that happen within its borders; we just care anyway, instinctively. But to advance this proposition is to forget that we automatically derive a sense of the ordinary on the basis of our day-to-day residence in our homeland. We know what it's like to take a train, attend a meeting, go to the shops, walk the children to school, flirt, laugh and get cross there – and this is why we immediately engage when we hear that someone has been kidnapped in Newcastle upon Tyne or that a bomb has exploded in Edgbaston.

The ideal news organization of the future, recognizing that an interest in the anomalous depends on a prior knowledge of the normal, would routinely commission stories on certain identification-inducing aspects of human nature which invariably exist even in the most far-flung and ravaged corners of our globe. Having learned something about street parties in Addis Ababa, love in Peru and in-laws in Mongolia, audiences would be prepared to care just a little more about the next devastating typhoon or violent coup.

6.

THERE IS ANOTHER assumption at work with regard to the ultimate purpose of foreign news coverage. As it currently exists, foreign reporting implicitly defers to the priorities of the state and of business, occupying itself almost exclusively with events which touch on military, commercial or humanitarian concerns. Foreign news wants to tell us with whom and where we should fight, trade or sympathize.

But these three areas of interest really aren't priorities for the majority of us. At a much deeper, more metaphysical level, foreign news should offer us a means by which to humanize the Other – that is, the outsider from over the mountains or beyond the seas who instinctively repels, bores or frightens us and with whom we can't, without help, imagine having anything in common. Foreign news should find ways to make us all more human in one another's eyes, so that the apparently insuperable barriers of geography, culture, race and class could be transcended and fellow feeling might develop across chasms.

Many a high-minded news organization has inveighed bitterly against those who resent the influx of immigrants from other countries. But this view proceeds from the assumption that a reflexive suspicion towards foreigners is a mark of Satan rather than a common, almost natural result of ignorance – a fault which news organizations have an explicit ability to reduce through a more imaginative kind of reporting (as opposed to ineffective, guilt-inducing denunciations of bigotry).

To achieve its stated objectives, foreign news should be willing to adopt some of the techniques of art. As George Eliot suggested, art as a medium is capable of helping us by 'amplifying experience and extending our contact with our fellow-men beyond the bounds of our personal lot'. Its greatest benefit, according to Eliot, is 'the extension of our sympathies'. Now more than ever, we need these sympathies to be extended, in part because so much of the information we receive comes at us as data or abstract facts which our deeper selves cannot digest ('East DR Congo Faces Catastrophic Humanitarian Crisis'). Eliot went on to note, 'Appeals founded on generalizations and statistics require a sympathy ready-made…; but a picture of human life such as a great artist can give, surprises even the trivial and the selfish into that attention to what is apart from themselves, which may be called the raw material of moral sentiment.'

This, in a nutshell, should be the task of foreign news: to foster our 'attention to what is apart from' us and thereby facilitate imaginative contact, practical assistance and mutual understanding between us and other populations.

A further, related psychological rationale of the news is to help us to recover perspective. Living in one society only, it is easy to forget to notice, let alone appreciate, the advantages of our particular civilization – the relative sophistication of our laws, social habits, educational traditions and transport networks. We can't see what has been so difficult to achieve. Foreign countries furnish a scale against which our own nation and ways of living can be assessed; they may help us to see our national oddities, blind spots and strengths. Stories from them may lead us to a fresh appreciation of the imperfect freedoms and comparative abundance of our homelands which otherwise would be treated only as matters for grumbling or blame. Alternatively, problems with which we are all too familiar may be revealed as having found better solutions elsewhere. Things that had seemed to be inevitable can emerge as cultural options, open to change.

It should be a task of the news to highlight the virtues and flaws of all that has become too present and too ubiquitous for us to see.

7.

SCEPTICS WILL ARGUE that we're being naive here, insisting that, except under particular circumstances, we can't really be expected to care about what is happening abroad. Foreign reportage will always bore us, this thesis holds, because we are at heart only ever interested in 'ourselves', a category whose limits are delineated by the strict confines of our families, our friends, our safety, our jobs and the weather over our heads. So if, for instance, we were to switch on the television and chance upon a news report about the latest goings-on within the Italian government (in the Senato della Repubblica in the Palazzo Madama in Rome, the budget process is again causing mayhem, old allegiances are fraying and new, more expedient alliances are being formed), we would inevitably yawn and change the channel.

But that cannot be the whole story, for our native curiosity is in actuality far more tenacious than this view would suggest. We are quite capable of being gripped by and even sobbing over the fates of individuals who lived, governed and died in foreign countries not just within our own lifetimes but hundreds or perhaps thousands of years ago, people who had odd names and odder occupations and whose actions had no direct consequences whatsoever upon our lives. We can sit in a darkened theatre for two and a quarter hours and give little thought to the interval as we closely follow the story of a praetor in ancient Rome named Marcus Brutus, who once heard some worrying news from his friend Gaius Cassius about plans that were being hatched in the Senate.

How is it that we can care about what happens in William Shakespeare's *Julius Caesar*? Why are we willing to expend our precious mental resources on something so remote from our own concerns? The answer is that even though this play is ostensibly about some peculiar political machinations on the Italian peninsula a couple of millennia ago, it is in truth, all along and simultaneously, actually about *us*.

Properly told, stories are able to operate on two levels. On the surface, they deal with *particulars* involving a range of facts related to a given time and place, a local culture and a social group – and it is these specifics that tend to bore us whenever they lie outside of

Political news
Important, and embarrassingly boring,
developments in the Italian Republic.

Julius Caesar
Important, and oddly fascinating,
developments in the Roman Republic.

our own experience. But then, a layer beneath the particulars, the *universals* are hidden: the psychological, social and political themes that transcend the stories' temporal and geographical settings and are founded on unvarying fundamentals of human nature.

In the language of particulars, Shakespeare's history play is 'about' ancient Rome, dramatizing the rather arcane events surrounding Caesar's triumphant return from waging war against Pompey, as Gaius Cassius plotted to murder him with the support of Marcus Brutus. But in the language of universals, *Julius Caesar* confronts timeless themes such as how we decide what we owe to our friends and what we should give to our country, how we should respond to rumours and plots and how we might distinguish between apprehension and panic. It looks at the way good intentions can usher in disastrous results and considers the roles played by error and blindness in the affairs even of decent men.

We can't expect the average news story to be written up with Shakespearean skill, but we might insist that it pay a degree of Shakespearean attention to universals, especially where the particulars are likely to seem off-puttingly foreign. There are ways of presenting a story that assist us in transferring knowledge across cultural and circumstantial gaps and in viewing the myriad experiences of our fellow human beings as resources on which we can continuously draw for inspiration, caution, guidance and insight.

8.

WE HAVEN'T LOST all our appetite for elsewhere. We are creatures who, in previous ages, stood in queues to hear tales about so-called exotic lands. The problem is that the reporting methodologies developed by the modern news media – which privilege factually accurate, technologically speedy, impersonal, crisis-focused coverage to the near exclusion of any other kind – have by error led to a sort of globalized provincialism, whereby we at once know a good deal and don't care about very much; whereby a little knowledge of the wrong kind has managed to narrow rather than expand the compass of our curiosity.

Yet our fascination and our empathy are merely slumbering. To become powerful once more, foreign news needs only to submit itself to some of the processes of art.

The Details

The Ugandan government auditor has reported that millions of dollars have been transferred from Prime Minister Amama Mbabazi's office into private accounts. Mr Mbabazi has acknowledged that money has been stolen from his office, but denies any involvement. The Ugandan President's adviser, John Nagenda, said the government was determined to ensure that those responsible for the alleged corruption were brought to justice. All Ugandans were 'absolutely fed up' with corruption, he said. Mr Mbabazi has denied wrongdoing, but acknowledges there has been 'massive theft' from his office. ¶

BBC

1.

DURING A VISIT to the BBC Uganda desk, while enjoying some banana cake that a colleague from BBC Nigeria had brought in and generously shared, I tried to hint as gently as I could at my inability to develop much of an interest in the news that the desk's staff were so assiduously collecting from their country and attempting to disseminate to an apathetic world – news which, on that particular day, included an account of the brazen theft of $12 million in aid money from the office of the Ugandan prime minister.

2.

AS FAR AS Ugandan political news went, this was clearly a matter of considerable significance, but on the BBC's website, the report had the misfortune of competing with, first, an item about a married footballer who had been photographed in the arms of the wife of one of Britain's most famous television chefs, and second, a piece about a French actress who had been injured, under peculiar circumstances, on the yacht of an American Internet billionaire as it lay moored off the coast of Monte Carlo. Predictably, the Uganda story stood little chance.

The BBC Uganda staffers were more gracious than they could by rights have been in the face of my and my society's lack of interest. Finally one of the team, a young Ugandan who had spent several years as a teenager in a refugee camp in the north of the country, suggested that the best thing might be for me actually to *go* to Uganda and see the place for myself, in the hope of perhaps igniting an interest that had eluded me thus far.

3.

AND SO I went; not because I wanted to, but precisely because I really didn't – and yet I wanted to understand why. I went to develop my ideas as to why so many foreign countries lack any appeal whatsoever to a dispiritingly large share of a home audience and what role the news might play in supporting or creating this lassitude and disengagement.

My first surprise was that I had to go on a journey to get to Uganda. Technology helps to mask this somewhat obvious detail. For most of human history, the obstacles presented by overseas travel and communication were so formidable that the geographical – and also by implication the psychological and cultural – distances between countries were constantly and automatically emphasized. To cross an ocean, or even to send a simple message, was an extraordinarily time-consuming and expensive feat which left everyone in sure command of a moral that has a tendency to get lost nowadays when, at the tap of a screen, we can – at no cost to us – travel at the speed of light through the undersea Internet cable SEA-ME-WE4 from Marseilles to Djibouti and then, via the East African undersea fibre-optic cable EASSy, from Mombasa to Kampala, from where we declare a feeling of boredom and impatience: a moral that the experiences of mankind are infinitely more complex and interesting than we could ever imagine when we gaze out from our own static narrow vantage point and that it is hence a basic courtesy we should pay to the planet and its many lands to remain at all times open, curious and modest before their manifold mysteries.

This moral would have stuck naturally in the mind when the only way to get to Uganda was to travel for two months by sea around the perilous Cape of Good Hope bound for Dar es Salaam, then inland for another few months through bush and desert, with every likelihood that one would never return. In 1859, John Hanning Speke, the first European ever to enter Uganda and the man who gave Lake Inyansha its new name, Lake Victoria, made it back to Britain and gave a lecture on his travels to an almost hysterical 800-strong crowd in the Royal Geographical Society in Kensington. For these people, there was no doubt that 'foreign news' was exciting in the extreme. Speke told them that near Lake Manyara, in Tanzania, he had been attacked by fierce local hunters and ended up with a javelin impaled through both his cheeks. A few days after, a beetle had crawled into his ear, had started gnawing at his eardrum and had eventually had to be scraped out with a knife. The moment when he finally ascended the lush tropical hills on which the city of Kampala now stands was evocatively described in the bestselling travel book he published in 1863, *The Discovery of the Source of the Nile*:

> We crossed over a low spur of hill and stretching as far as the eye could reach was a rich, well-wooded, land-scape. I was immensely struck with the neatness and good arrangement of the place, as well as its excessive beauty and richness. No part of Bengal or Zanzibar could excel it in either respect; and my men, with one voice, exclaimed, 'Ah, what people these are!' …
> I felt inclined to stop here a month, everything was so pleasant … The whole land was a picture of qui-escent beauty, with the boundless [Lake Victoria] in the background … At night a hyena came into my

hut, and carried off one of my goats that was tied to
a log between two of my sleeping men …

There was little danger that the original audience for this sort
of material was going to be distracted by the nineteenth-century
equivalent of an anecdote about a philandering footballer.

Even now, the journey down to Uganda is hardly a jaunt: the
eight-hour flight in a Boeing 767, spanning some 6,500 kilometres
between London and Entebbe, serves as an appropriately powerful
reminder of the scale of our planet. Six hours in and you start flying
over the endless ochre desert near Ounianga Kébir in Chad. Europe
is far away now. An hour later, the boredom interminable, you riffle
once again through the in-flight magazine while the plane enters
the airspace over North Sudan. On the airline's route map, the
names themselves are charged and oddly poetic – Emi Koussi, Am
Djeress, Umm Buru, Muhajiriya – so many unforeseen, unknown
locations that are home to people whose assumptions and ways
of life would be deeply challenging if the plane were to choose to
fail at this point. Now comes a snack assembled late last night in
Hounslow (a choice of a cheese or egg and cress sandwich) to be
eaten in the minutes between Khogali and Tambura, a journey
between two towns that would take five days on foot. Eventually,
over the Democratic Republic of Congo, the seat-belt signs come
on, there is a thanks from the captain, a reminder about immigration and malaria, and then a descent over Hoima and Luwero to
Entebbe, with, as a backdrop, Lake Victoria sunk in tarry darkness
punctuated by the flickering lamps of hundreds of tiny fishing boats.

We are wary of anything 'exotic' now. This way of prais-
ing what is foreign seems dangerously provincial, patronizing and

possibly racist. Foreign news has actively distanced itself from travel writing and all the accompanying paraphernalia of exoticism. Cautious neither to overpraise nor to denigrate other cultures, it has settled as a compromise on a permanently neutral tone, never expressing any wonder at the ways or practices of the far-flung corners of the world it reports from. It never seems amazed to find itself where it is; it simply accepts without astonishment or explicit comment that it is filing a story from a spot where brides offer their grooms a goat on their marriage day, where there may be *luwombo* with *sim-sim* paste for supper and where it can be 30 degrees centigrade in the shade at midday, none of which is apparently interesting when the news could be focusing on the prime minister's likely role in an incident of financial maladministration.

Nevertheless, upon landing in Uganda, one can't help but be struck by what still deserves to be recognized as exotic: by the colourful adverts for Bidco's Golden Fry Superior Vegetable Oil hand-painted on the sides of houses, by the names of one's new acquaintances (Patience, Ignatius and Kenneth), by the smells of roasting meat and campfire smoke, by the marabous, the weaver birds and the turacos that wheel in the light-blue morning sky and perch on the tops of the telecom masts, by the fig trees that grow in the middle of traffic islands, and everywhere by the constant repetition, at moments of delay (of which there are many), of the old Ugandan proverb '*Mpola mpola, otuuka waala*' (a version of 'Make haste slowly').

The news is keen never to sound remotely like him.
John Hanning Speke (1827–64).

4.

IN TRAVEL LITERATURE, we enter foreign nations with the help of narrators with whom we can identify and who respond to other countries with some of the assumptions and fears we ourselves might harbour. They, too, might miss home and get frightened of fevers and bugs. They, too, might admit to weakness, excitement and despair. They, too, might flinch a little from their normal journalistic impassivity upon seeing, along the main road leading into Kampala, a large and unconvincing sign bearing the promise that 'Together we can kill Marburg Disease' (a highly contagious haemorrhagic fever virus which proves fatal to over 80 per cent of its victims within two days and is endemic throughout large sections of Uganda).

Nowadays, though, any kind of personal narrator would be deemed an intrusion on the objectivity of reporting. Foreign news hence avoids speaking to us with any kind of voice or personality. Yet if any harm could conceivably come to a viewer from seeing another country through the distorting lens of a correspondent who expressed candid reactions to it, it is as nothing next to what can be the stifling boredom produced by ostensibly neutral and accurate reporters who, by their implicit denial of even having a response to anything foreign, fatally undermine our desire to add to our knowledge of the world.

5.

IN THE RUSH to acquaint us with the so-called 'main events', the news forgets that our sense of engagement with a country depends on our being shown those smaller visual or sensory elements which alone can excite our deeper interest in a people and a place. If we are going to feel any real concern about Ugandan news we will first need to know something about the mango trees in Kampala, whose sweet smells drift across the crowded boulevards after the almost hourly tropical showers. It helps to look around a typical Kampala office, to see how the country's schools work, to learn about relationship rituals and to browse the local newspaper, *New Vision*, and take in reports of the latest crimes:

> Former Medical Union president Dr. Apollo Nyangasi has been sentenced to life imprisonment after being found guilty of killing his wife Christine following wrangles over property. Delivering her judgment on Wednesday, High Court Judge, Jane Kiggundu said Nyangasi's actions were uncivilized. Nyangasi committed the offence on July 24, 2010, at their marital home in Kireka Kira division in Wakiso district. The couple had been married for 17 years and has two children. The state attorney had asked the court to pass the death sentence against Nyangasi on grounds that he killed his wife in a brutal manner. ¶

The very tone of this account points up some of the distance we have travelled. The judge deemed it merely 'uncivilized' for a man to kill his wife, and the state attorney argued for capital punishment not as a fitting penalty for murder per se but because, instead of dispatching her using some kinder method, Apollo had killed Christine 'in a brutal manner'. The 'wrangles' over property sound confoundingly sedate as well ('We were having wrangles so I hammered her to death…'). Without quite meaning to, the article conveys an unusual world in which violence is always close to the surface as a behavioural option, as a response to frustration and inconvenience, and where mayhem is such a constant and overwhelming threat that the local news media, unlike their sensationalizing counterparts in more law-abiding countries, can address it only in the most squeamish euphemisms.

6.

I ACCOMPANY THE BBC's correspondent to a press conference with the embattled prime minister, who for several weeks now has faced accusations from foreign governments, as well as from many of his own people, of being a thief. From such occasions, the news machine demands one thing above all: a quote of around fifty words, subsequently to be complemented by another fifty words from an opposition spokesman.

But even this journalistic set piece provides the bystander with an opportunity to learn about Uganda in non-standard ways – for example, by studying the very large photograph, remarkably still on prominent display, of the prime minister embracing Colonel Muammar Gaddafi at the African Union gathering in Kampala in 2010 (the last such event the colonel attended); or by noting, around the conference table, the gigantic black leather swivelling chairs, 1970s in style, a porn-film director's idea of a seat fit for an important CEO, on which the prime minister and his aides are enthroned.

Stuart Franklin, *The Prime Minister of Uganda*, 2012.

Stuart Franklin, *Lobby of the Serena Hotel, Kampala*, 2004.

There is something to be learned about Uganda, too, from our host's unswerving refusal to give any kind of answer conforming to the norms of contemporary journalism. On being asked if the allegations against him have prompted him to think of resigning, he offers a slow, wounded smile and a theatrically circumlocutory reply which seems oddly to combine the English diction of a Southern Baptist preacher with the sombre tone of an executioner (indeed, he ran the security services for many years). 'My friends,' he begins, 'dear friends, all of you here are my friends; we in Uganda reach out to the world with a hand of friendship. So to all of you gathered here today, enough of distrust and sadness, enough of blame. The certainty is that no bad thing will befall us again in the future that we are building for Ugandans, all Ugandans, the very poor as well as those who have come by prosperity, today and tomorrow and every day that the Lord grants us.' Certainly not the sort of statement that can be tidily shoehorned into the next bulletin.

If news stories have their accepted norms, so, too, do the photographs that are used to illustrate them. Convention demands head shots at desks, officials-disembarking-from-a-plane shots, men-at-podium shots – nothing too idiosyncratic and certainly nothing too 'artistic'. And yet there is something to be gained if the photographer who has come out to Kampala with the author breaks the rules in order to capture both the shocked look in the prime minister's eyes in the split second after he is asked a blunt question by a reporter and the female assistant whom he has instructed to record *us* while we record *him*, perhaps as an implicit reminder that he holds the keys to the torture cells situated, according to Amnesty International, in the basement of the building we are in.

Stuart Franklin,
Brass Instruments, Independence Celebrations, Hoima, Uganda, 2012.

Good photographs compress extended themes into single images: they can speak of the whole nation's endemic corruption simply by showing us a few men waiting idly in the lobby of a luxury hotel, or of its extreme poverty by focusing on a musician's battered tuba at a parade celebrating (though that might not be quite the word for it) the fiftieth anniversary of Ugandan independence.

7.

IN HIS POEM 'Asphodel, That Greeny Flower' (1955), the American poet William Carlos Williams famously wrote:

> It is difficult
> to get the news from poems
> yet men die miserably every day
> for lack
> of what is found there.

The bit about 'dying' is, naturally, an overstatement. What Williams fears is that without regular contact with poetry, we may lose our vitality, cease to understand ourselves, neglect our powers of empathy or become unimaginative, brittle and sterile. Literature, for Williams as for George Eliot before him, is the medium that can reawaken us to the world. The news may have an intense surface seriousness – which sensible people naturally imagine gives it a greater claim over our attention than verse could ever hope to command – but the artist recognizes its dangerously anaesthetizing effects.

Pupil of Pieter Bruegel the Elder, *Landscape with the Fall of Icarus*, c. 1565.

Yet this equation – poetry as life, news as death – is no permanent law; it isn't the category of 'news' itself that is at fault, for in its essence the word doesn't signify anything more specific than that which is happening in the world at a given moment. It isn't news per se that is the problem, only the 'life'-inhibiting version of it that too often abounds. However, if Tolstoy, Flaubert or Sophocles were in the newsroom, the medium might well give us rather more of what we need in order to keep our souls from 'dying', for what were *War and Peace*, *Madame Bovary* and *Antigone* in their original state but just the things that William Carlos Williams so unfairly attacked – namely, news events?

8.

SOME SIXTEEN YEARS before the publication of 'Asphodel', W. H. Auden had taken his readers to Brussels in his own poem 'Musée des Beaux Arts', placing them in front of *Landscape with the Fall of Icarus*, a painting long thought to be by Bruegel but now attributed to one of his pupils.

The painting shows us a superficially bucolic scene: ships are taking sail, a shepherd is tending to his flock, distant cities look prosperous and ordered. But in the bottom right-hand corner of the canvas, a tragedy is unfolding all but unheeded (the headlines, had there been any, would have been about something else that day): reckless Icarus, having allowed the sun to melt the wax of his homemade wings, has just tumbled into the sea, to his death. A resolute ploughman at the centre of the picture references a popular proverb, 'No plough stops for the dying man.'

The detail.

Not many people have noticed Icarus – but the painter and now the poet have. This, Auden wants to tell us, is what artists *do*: they notice stuff; the small and unobtrusive stuff that other people – ploughmen and shepherds, you and me, and journalists in a hurry – miss and yet that is essential to halting our usual indifference and callousness.

9.

WE NEED A kind of foreign news that hangs more tenaciously on the details, a news that ignites our interest in events by remaining open to some of the lessons of art, a news that lets the poets, the travel writers and the novelists impart aspects of their crafts to journalists – and perhaps occasionally even lets them have a desk of their own somewhere in the quieter corners of the newsroom – so that we won't so regularly be able to walk blithely past the planet's less obtrusive beauty and tragedy.

Photography

A generic President Barack Obama (Getty Images).

I.

THERE IS NO more oppressed or put-upon figure in the newsrooms of the modern world than the photo editor. Responsible for coordinating the visual aspect of news output, the men and women who fill this position almost always repeat (out of earshot of their bosses) the identical complaint: 'No one believes in photography any more.'

This is not to say that no photographs are employed to illustrate the news; far from it. There are now more images than ever before embedded in the coverage we consume. The problem lies in the lack of ambition behind their production and display. Photographs are still used, but the arguments for taking, identifying and then paying for the best examples appear to have been forgotten. A great majority of the pictures that do make it into print are compressed, bland, repetitive, clichéd and sidelined, and are seen, unsurprisingly, as nothing more than blocks of colour that can break up monochromatic runs of text.

We might usefully divide news photographs into two genres. The first are images of *corroboration*, which do little other than confirm something we have learned about a person or an event through an accompanying article. So if a story informs us that the president gave a speech, a photograph will appear to one side verifying just this. The idea here is that photography should just furnish an extra level of proof as to the reality of events which have already been described in language.

Then there is another, rarer kind of image, the photograph of *revelation*, whose ambition is not simply to back up what the text tells us but to *advance* our level of knowledge to a new point. It sets out to challenge cliché.

Anonymous, *Portrait of Henri IV*, 17th century.

Jean-Auguste-Dominique Ingres,
Henri IV Receiving the Ambassador of Spain, 1817.

If photo editors can seem a little defeated, it is because they have daily to confront the fact that the photographs demanded and paid for by their industry almost always fall into the first, cheaper and less useful of these two categories.

2.

A SIMILAR DICHOTOMY between images that corroborate and ones that reveal can be found in the fine arts, and particularly in portraiture and history paintings. We might compare, for instance, two rather different pictures of Henri IV, king of France. In the first, by an unknown seventeenth-century painter, the monarch looks kindly, stiff and opaque. We can take it on faith that this is a fair enough likeness, but the portrait does little to enhance our knowledge of the king's nature. Contrast this with an early-nineteenth-century painting by Ingres in which Henri is shown sprawled on the floor with his children, pretending to be a horse or perhaps a donkey. On the left side of the canvas, the Spanish ambassador has just arrived to see him, but the king is asking for a few minutes more to finish his game. Ingres's image goes beyond just confirming that Henri existed and that he had a beard: it invites us to consider a statesman's soul.

3.

EVERY GREAT NEWS image should likewise enrich our otherwise deficient and prejudiced pictures of reality.

For example, I thought I knew about child marriages, but until I saw a photograph taken by Stephanie Sinclair, I had never realized that the young brides involved aren't really children. Marriage swiftly turns them into diminutive old ladies, with expressions at once resigned, solemn, betrayed and infinitely sad. In tandem, their husbands are not the mature brutes I imagined

Stephanie Sinclair, *Tahani and Ghada, Yemen*, 2010.

them to be. They look guileless, innocent and confused, seemingly still children themselves. It is almost beyond imagining that these poignant, absurd, cursed pairs of spouses could even begin to offer each other comfort.

I thought I knew that war wasn't generally a good idea and that innocents sometimes got killed in crossfire, but I didn't realize quite how much I also believed in every attempt at diplomacy and quite how much I wouldn't mind if some rather important strategic interests were lost so long as war could be avoided – and fathers didn't have to mourn their blood-soaked sons.

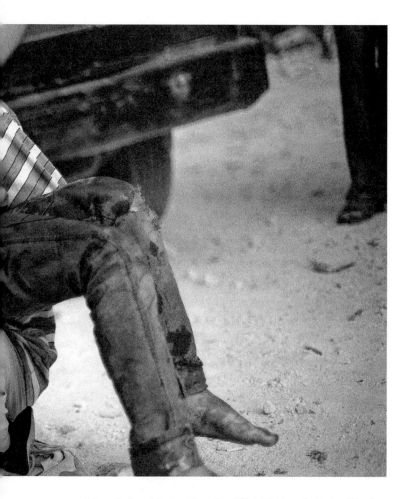

Manu Brabo, *A Syrian Man Cries While Holding the Body of His Son, Killed by the Syrian Army, near Dar El Shifa Hospital in Aleppo, Syria*, 2012.

I thought I knew about the world, but I realize now that despite the countless photos I have seen and the many publications I have read, I retain barely a single image in my imagination of most countries around our planet. I struggle to summon up any visual associations whatsoever with Chile or Peru, I have no clue what Burundi or Niger looks like, I can't picture Burkina Faso or the

Stuart Franklin, *Streetlife, Kinshasa*, 2004.

Solomon Islands – and so I am fascinated by a photograph that at least teaches me that in Kinshasa shops sell household goods, people speak French ('*Vente des Appareils Electroménager*') and young men, whatever troubles they may have seen, still know something about laughter and play.

I thought I knew about President Obama, too, because I have seen him in a great many photographs giving speeches against the backdrop of the presidential eagle. I knew that he was capable of faking certain things to get elected, but I didn't realize that he could also, in his better moments, fake a thing or two to please a child. I therefore stare for a long time at an image taken by the

Pete Souza, *President Barack Obama Pretends to Be Caught in Spider-Man's Web as He Greets the Son of a White House Staffer in the Outer Oval Office*, 2012.

White House staff photographer, Pete Souza, thinking that Obama, like his counterpart Henri IV four centuries back, may be at his most touchingly powerful precisely when he lets himself be the playmate of a child.

4.

AS READERS OF news stories, we have seen so many bad photographs that it is unlikely even to occur to us that it might be rewarding occasionally to stop and look properly at a few of their good counterparts. It would seem bizarre to interrupt the reading of an article in order to contemplate an accompanying image for as long as we might study a painting in a museum – say, thirty seconds or more – and with an expectation of learning something distinctive. We have lost any sense of photography's potential as an information-bearing medium, as a force with a crucial job to do in terms of properly introducing us to a planet that we keep conceitedly and recklessly assuming that we know rather well already.

IV.

Economics

M2 and Utopia

South Korea's M2, a narrow measure of the money supply, rose 4.6 percent on-year to 1,827.3 trillion won in October, slowing from a 5.2 percent on-year gain in September, according to the Bank of Korea (BOK). On a seasonally adjusted basis, the country's M2 grew 0.2 percent in October from the previous month, picking up from a 0.1 percent on-month gain in September. South Korea's liquidity aggregate, the broadest measure of the money supply, grew 7.8 percent in October from the previous year, down from the 8.9 percent on-year gain in September, the BOK added. ❡

Yonhap News, Korea

I.

IN ITS MORE serious moods, the news seeks to explain the world to us, which means attempting to sift through the dramas, hyperbole and clamour of every new day in order to direct our attention to the handful of developments that could turn out truly to matter. There is so much we might find engaging (a couple has jumped off the Golden Gate Bridge; several bits of Tasmania are on fire; a Mexican industrialist has shot and killed a rival), but what in the news is really worth focusing on?

We are the inheritors of an idea, endorsed by both the right and the left wings of the political spectrum, that the most fundamental reality of nations is their financial state – and that economic reporting should therefore be recognized as the most important facet of all news output.

2.

IN THE MORE ambitious news outlets, our eyes are regularly directed towards a variety of key indicators on the economic dashboard, including the money supply (M1, M2, MZM), central bank reserves, factory orders, the consumer price index (CPI), building permits, jobless claims, the deficit, the national debt and, most significantly of all, the GDP.

The numbers can be disorientating. To assess a nation through its economic data is a little like re-envisaging oneself via the results of a blood test, whereby the traditional markers of personality and character are set aside and it is made clear that one is at base, where it really counts, a creatinine level of 3.2, a lactate dehydrogenase of 927, a leukocyte (per field) of 2 and a C-reactive protein of 2.42.

Like blood to a human, money is to the state the constantly circulating, life-giving medium in which some of the most telling data about the future is carried in encoded forms. Sampling it is the task of the great government financial labs: the Office of National Statistics in Britain, the Department of Commerce in the United States, L'Institut National de la Statistique et des Etudes Economiques in France and the National Statistical Office of South Korea. Every week, their statisticians will survey the economy; in the UK alone, taking in data from 6,000 companies in the manufacturing sector, 25,000 service firms, 5,000 retailers, 10,000 construction businesses and 4,000 government projects in agriculture, energy, health and education. With gigantic computers helping them to process their harvest of information, the statisticians will publish some astonishingly abbreviated yet deeply resonant findings. The GDP figures might, for example, inform us that the financial value of all work done across the entire country over the previous quarter had risen 1.1 per cent or (heaven forbid) dropped 0.5 per cent, figures beneath which will lie tens of thousands of meetings, anxieties, quandaries, ploys, boardroom discussions, early morning commutes, sackings, initiatives, launches and disappointments, all now harnessed to and confined within a mere two digits.

Distillation is familiar from other areas of science – the discipline to which economics aspires. In chemistry, too, we are invited to look beneath the confusion of physical reality to uncover a mere 118 elements which underlie matter and can, with an almost artistic grace, be ranked according to their chemical properties, atomic numbers and electron configurations into the columns of the periodic table.

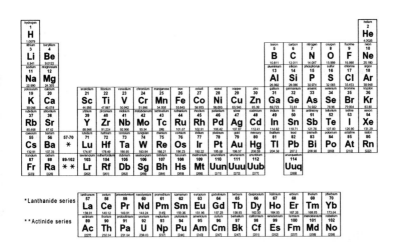

Everything out there (the trees, your spouse, the office) is, at heart, this.

3.

ECONOMIC DATA CAN rupture the sense of scale we ordinarily rely on to make our lives feel meaningful or hopeful. Our sense of purpose can be crushed by the unimaginable dimensions of the system in which economics reveals us to exist: one where world GDP stands at $70,000,000,000,000, where the global bond market is worth $100 trillion and the derivatives market $791 trillion, where world debt is measured at $50 trillion, EU debt at $17 trillion and US debt at $16 trillion (spending a dollar a second, a trillion dollars would take 31,000 years to run through); where a billion people live in poverty while an elite made up of the wealthiest 2 per cent owns more than half of all wealth. Such figures have some of the numbing quality of the statistics of astronomy, when it informs us that the Milky Way contains 400 billion stars or that it would take 93 billion light years to cross the universe. Our minds are not well fitted to contemplate our condition from such perspectives. Our aspirations become laughable, if not absurd, played out against such a canvas. We grow newly humble and supine before a sense of our utter nothingness.

4.

IT ISN'T ONLY the scale of the economic machine that can silence us, but also its complexity. Only a minuscule percentage of the populations of developed economies have any solid understanding of the workings of the economic system they exist within. Most of us will struggle to grasp quite what might be going on within essential terms like arbitrage, Basel 1 and 2, cyclically adjusted current budgets, price/earnings ratios or quantitative easing. As we follow financial events in the news, we may ask, and not for the first time: 'What *is* the growth rate of money?' 'How do hedge funds operate?' 'What does the LIBOR rate determine?' 'What is liquidity?' 'How does inflation targeting work?' 'How can a government "print money" and what are the long-term consequences?'

Those kindly commentators occasionally employed by news organizations to help us with our confusions certainly try hard to offer us explanations, but perhaps because the concepts that dizzy us lack connection with anything in our day-to-day lives, their explanations have a habit of leaching from our minds just hours after we have heard them.

If we really want to take matters in hand and educate ourselves about the details, we must have steady nerves. Consider, for example, the rationale normally given for the equation of exchange, a concept that is situated in the gentlest foothills of economic science but that already asks us to contemplate a scenario in which

$$M \cdot V_T = \sum_i (p_i \cdot q_i) = p^T \cdot q$$

and where:

p_i and q_i are the respective price and quantity
of the i-th transaction
p^T is a row vector of the p_i
q is a column vector of the q_i

– by which point most of us will be itching to run away, perhaps back to the tragic news story of the couple who jumped off the Golden Gate Bridge.

In certain moods, we may feel almost agreeably small before the majesty and intricacy of economics. In their field, theologians sometimes describe a feeling of awe that can result when the tiny human ego is confronted by the divine presence and experiences what is termed in Latin the *mysterium tremendum*, the mystery of the divine. There may be comparable moments of *mysterium tremendum* when the mind comes up against a dispersion output graph:

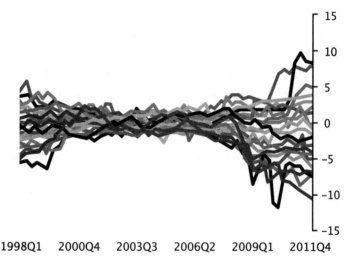

Dispersion output graph.

5.

WHILE WE MAY sometimes willingly defer to the greater intelligence of economics, in other moods it can be hard to quell certain rebellious questions which arise when we contemplate the economic arrangements of the planet as they are relayed to us by the news.

Lying awake at night, for instance, some of us may wonder, in a sincere and yet inarticulate way, why it is that the world built by capitalism is not (bathos intended) *nicer*. Why is there still so much suffering all around? Why do some have so much and others so little? Why are most jobs mindless? Why can't there be more security and leisure? Why do anxiety and fear persist almost everywhere? Aren't we destroying the planet for no particular reason or reward? (By this time it may be getting very late, and only a stubborn few will continue to press on.) Couldn't we start again in some new way, rejig things, perhaps pass some laws and experiment with bold new ideas in order to create a freer, less anxious, *happier* world?

6.

WE KNOW WELL enough that these aren't serious questions; they are the sorts of things that fourteen-year-olds write poems about or argue with their parents over. In the morning, we'll put them firmly away. They don't belong to the standard narrative of economics in the news. We may blanch to think of what any properly intelligent and sensible person might make of them – someone like, say, the chairman of the Federal Reserve, the most powerful economist in the world today.

If our questions seem immature, it is because we associate maturity with a sober acceptance of a great many things that are painful but necessary for the functioning of economic life, whereas our musings sound like the reality-denying ravings of a utopian dreamer. Adulthood involves learning to conclusively bury a great many of our hopes. Standard economics honours this process of growing up and the accompanying masochism required; it is mostly a story of pain, teaching us a lot of complicated but sound reasons why a great many nice things aren't possible: why we can't wave a magic wand and make poor countries rich; why competition and therefore anxiety are necessary in a market economy; why total job security makes people lazy; why a country has to reward its winners and punish its losers; why rich people can't be proportionately taxed; why we can't all live more simply yet still with dignity; why governments can't limit the free market in the name of higher values; why inane consumer goods are an indispensable part of a flourishing economy; why it's good for growth if people don't generally share and recycle their belongings and why we can't afford too intense a concern for making the world beautiful and clean.

7.

WE END UP with the following situation: on the one hand, we have a news agenda dominated by reports of the workings of a highly complicated social science that wrestles with problems of near cosmic scale and incomprehensible difficulty, upon which it periodically delivers pronouncements at once pessimistic and resigned; and on the other hand, we have a host of inchoate, naive, innocent, impassioned but powerful longings that are carefully concealed and mostly go unmentioned for fear of sacrificing claims to decency and adult seriousness.

8.

OCCASIONALLY, THE TENSIONS get too much and there are explosions. A group of people collectively declare that they've had enough, paint some placards, buy megaphones and take their positions outside the central bank, the fast-food concession or the oil company headquarters. A few weeks later, after some moments of exuberance and struggles with heavy-handed police, the makeshift camps are hosed down and the news moves on.

These explosions are undermined by a fatal naivety: that is, by a set of the best possible intentions to improve a problematic situation – combined with a lack of any effective or forensic knowledge about what has caused it in the first place. A complaint that might have occasioned an intricate political argument instead ends up as a primal scream.

9.

THE NEWS IS partly to blame for this incoherent rage; it is the news that helps to raise audiences that cannot make sense of and feel hopeless about their condition and that are fed a diet of economic analyses that skilfully crushes ambitious considerations of how to create a more equitable world.

Occupy Wall Street, New York, September 2011.

The protesters rightly recognize that there are things wrong with the economic system, but they find it hard to zero in on the specifics of the difficulties. It would take concentrated periods of guided interrogation and study to understand the mechanics of the financial machine – as well as to lay a finger on the realistic options for its reform. Tantalizingly, there are a great many very sensible options out there – which, non-coincidentally, we never hear about in the news for very long.

Most news is disinclined to provide a proper economic education equipped with a robust political dimension, either because it is itself confused and distracted about or because it benefits from the status quo.

It isn't the task or within the power of news to solve economic conundrums by itself. Its power is more secondary, and yet still it is considerable: the news has the ability to define the agenda, by leading the attention of an audience to what it believes to be the issues of importance, and then it can deliver an interested and knowledgeable constituency to governments and corporations.

At present, mainstream news organizations chiefly track the day-to-day activities within the economic establishment. They tell us what is going on, but not with any conviction of what might or should happen. In so far as the news creates an agenda, it is a limited one: whether one should intervene to bolster the labour market or not, leave or join the currency union, remain strict about inflation or be less vigilant. The economic 'debate' as it is seen through the lens of the news does not stray beyond tightly defined lines which restrict both an audience's expectations and its sense of what might be possible. Depart from the agenda (ask about reconceiving what a shareholder is and should be, for example, or question assumptions about growth and well-being) and, with bewildering speed, one ends up in territory deemed 'radical' and therefore ridiculous – even if most of what we now take for granted (a minimum wage, child protection, environmental legislation) started off by seeming entirely radical, if not insane, to 'sensible' opinion.

A perfect news service would analyse current events, but also convey a bold sense of the economic principles that should ideally underpin society. It would be guided by a sense of where one should be going, operating with an economic Utopia in mind, a community both prosperous and civilized, concerned as much with money as with its proper ends: fulfilment, fairness, generosity, beauty and kindness. It would be doctrinaire only about the destination, while remaining empirically flexible about the means of getting there – unlike right- and left-wing analyses that grow brittle and tiring through their axiomatic support of predictable means.

10.

WHILE CONTINUING ITS regular routine of analysing derivatives, yield ratios and the state of M2, economic news should not forget its ultimate responsibility to a larger quest for a world capable of sustaining less anxious and ruinous, more secure and more meaningful working lives.

Such an agenda, however fey it sounds within the context of classical economics, is at this point in our history too significant to be stumblingly raised only in private in the middle of the night or else shouted in a hoarse voice from a megaphone seconds before a police charge.

Investor News

Procter & Gamble Co. (PG), the world's largest consumer-products company, is closing hair-care research centers in the U.K. and Japan. The operations in Kobe, Japan, will move to Singapore, and work from the facility in Egham, England, will be moved to the U.S. The U.K. facility works on styling products, and the Japan site focuses on conditioners. P&G also operates a shampoo research center in Cincinnati and a coloring facility in Germany. P&G rose 0.7 percent to $69.82 at the close in New York. ¶

Bloomberg

I.

MANY OF THE wealthiest news organizations around the world spend the majority of their time turning out stories about what is happening inside individual companies. They cover developments within the automotive, aviation, energy, health, consumer, media and tech sectors, their focus powerfully directed by the demands of one kind of audience in particular: investors who need immediate and accurate data about the commercial fortunes of businesses to help them to determine where and how they should park their assets to grow their wealth.

Historically, the evolution of the modern news media has been closely linked to the need for market information on the part of capitalism's banks, brokerages and trading houses. The transoceanic cables laid between the United Kingdom and the United States in the mid-nineteenth century were jointly funded by financiers and news companies (Reuters, for one). Back then, in the depths of the glacial Atlantic waters, the news stories that ran down the cables would bear answers to such questions as: 'Is the demand for guano rising or falling?' 'What impact will a strike of silk weavers in Lyons have on the market for cotton?' 'How much revenue might be raised through a tax on malt?' And 'What might happen to corn prices if import restrictions were to be lifted?'

The emphasis on 'investor news' persists today. Even mainstream news organizations will give over prominent space to the latest numbers from the main stock markets around the world, along with real-time updates on the rising or falling fortunes of hundreds of thousands of little-known but evidently vast and important corporations which invisibly shore up our lives, from

Stocks & Indexes

Index Name	Value	Change
FTSE 100	6081.95	+17.37
Dow Jones	13384.29	-50.92
Nasdaq	3098.81	-2.85
Dax	7748.03	+15.37
Cac 40	3729.26	+24.62
S&P 500	1461.89	-4.58

Company	Value	Change	%
Nationstar Mortgage Holdings Inc.	38.83	+5.60	+16.85
Molycorp Inc.	11.56	+1.26	+12.23
Energysolutions Inc.	3.73	+0.29	+8.43
Newcastle Inv Corp.	9.60	+0.61	+6.79
Alcatel-Lucent SA ADR	1.73	+0.09	+5.49
Imax Corp.	24.08	+1.24	+5.43
Ocwen Financial Corp.	36.77	+1.88	+5.39
Quiksilver Corp.	5.29	+0.22	+4.34
Walter Industries Inc.	39.61	+1.59	+4.18
Sphere Drake Holdings Ltd.	6.80	+0.24	+3.66

What happened today, according to Bloomberg.

Molycorp Inc. (rare metals) to Sphere Drake Holdings Ltd (commercial property insurance).

2.

INVESTORS COME TO these news items with concentrated intent: when they consider a company, they want to see the figures for its five-year dividend growth, its latest earnings announcement, its price-to-book ratio for the most recent quarter (MRQ), market cap and current price-to-earnings (P/E) ratio (for the 'trailing twelve months', or TTM). At a pinch, they may also check its thirty-day average volume and relative P/E versus SPX.

But it is definitely outside of their remit to wonder what it might be like to be a sales representative or a factory supervisor at the company; to think about the tenor of the management, to imagine the cafeteria, to picture the manufacturing facilities in Shijiazhuang, to wonder about the origins of the raw materials or to ask what the point of a business might be in the wider human scheme.

Investors are like pilots flying high over a landscape at night. For navigation, they rely on only a few beacon signals and visual cues: the nuclear power station on the peninsula, the main north–south motorway and the medieval city, glowing like an encrusted diamond ring at the foot of the mountains. But there is no need to worry about the discussions in the apartment block near the piazza; the dilemmas of the lorry driver at the service station or the dreams of the technician in the turbine hall. In the cockpit, the only sounds are those of the twin Pratt & Whitney engines, thrumming at 25,000 rpms.

The financial news organizations have journalists embedded in some of the world's most remote economic outposts. There are correspondents monitoring the wheat harvest in Saskatchewan, Canada, the progress of oil exploration off the coast of Brazil, the extraction of niobium and zirconolite tantalum in Malawi, the development of the next generation of commuter trains in the Ruhr Valley, Germany, the weaving of carbon-fibre aerospace panels in Chubu, central Japan – and yet in spite of their extraordinary and privileged vantage points, these journalists are required to maintain a pinpoint focus on only such information as will help investors to answer one lone question: 'To which companies should we commit our money?'

3.

YET TO WRITE up the goings-on in businesses only in economic terms, to sum up an entire company as being +1.20 or to compress the experiences of 8,000 people into a turnover of 375.776 seems as limited as reducing a novel of the complexity of *Pride and Prejudice* to a ledger of the characters' bank accounts. Businesses should be honoured as among the most humanly important organizations on the planet which deserve to have their adventures, prevarications, deceits, passions and sufferings carefully described and powerfully evoked with all the intensity and aesthetic skill that might accompany the narration of a love affair. It is only an accident of culture that still leads us to expect that 'human interest' is something best found in someone's private life rather than at the factory line, the supply chain or the office cubicle. Because of its strict remit, investor news daily ignores phenomena that are no less involving, shocking, attractive and dramatic than what the show-business pages or a novel could offer us.

The journalists who work in the sector should demand that they be allowed to land the plane and add life to their numbers.

SHARP CORP.
TOKYO STOCK EXCHANGE
PRICE CHANGE: ¥-18
OPEN: ¥288 CLOSE: ¥270

They should, for example, be allowed to tell us more about fear. The layman meets the corporate world through fingerprint-free products that omit any mention of the circumstances behind their manufacture. Sharp's Aquos LE836 television or its R98STM-AA 900-watt microwave is deeply reserved about its origins in a factory on the southern outskirts of the town of Taki in Japan's Mie Prefecture. These supremely rational, well-engineered machines don't want to talk about the dynamics that brought them into being: the feelings of pride, jealousy, desire, cruelty and revenge that drove their creators on. Most of all, they don't want to speak of the anxiety that pervades capitalism in general and the 46,000 employees of Sharp in particular. 'Creative destruction' is a useful abstract phrase that financiers and economists will employ to describe the annihilation of weaker firms in a competitive marketplace, but what this means in reality, on the ground in Mie Prefecture, is the brutal end to decades of careful labour, effort, planning, energy and hope. We should dare to hear more about the constricted heart vessels and night-time agonies of Mikio Katayama, the chairman of Sharp Corp., an honourable and intelligent man who nevertheless made a few very bad bets – an investment in the wrong kind of flat-panel technology, a gamble on a second-rate smartphone screen, an overcommitment to microwaves just as the market turned – and who will now almost certainly be wiped out by the assaults of rival manufacturers, along with many of his co-workers and the value of his share price.

NESTLE SA
SWISS STOCK EXCHANGE
PRICE CHANGE: CHF +0.20
OPEN: CHF 63.55 CLOSE: CHF 63.75

We should at the same time be allowed to *see* the world behind the numbers, to appreciate capitalism as a visual, sensory phenomenon and to absorb the fearsomely ordered, sterile beauty of its offices and manufacturing centres. We should follow the photographer Jacqueline Hassink into the world's boardrooms, where decisions affecting the livelihoods of hundreds of thousands are taken amid stark but expensive furnishings by a few diligent courtiers, often engineers by training, masters of political intrigue and vessels for tightly coiled ambition – figures who somehow seem, in Hassink's images, all the more present and powerful for being absent. In the boardroom at Nestlé, near Geneva, for instance, we might briefly admire the map of our planet that allows the members of senior management, like generals in some previous age when war enjoyed the same prestige now accorded to business, to survey the relentless progress of their campaigns to advance the sales of Honey Nut Cheerios, San Pellegrino and Friskies to humans and cats across five continents.

Jacqueline Hassink, *The Meeting Table of the Board of Directors of Nestlé,
Vevey, Switzerland*, 1994.

Edward Burtynsky, *Cankun Factory, Xiamen City*, 2005.

TSANN KUEN ENTERPRISE CO. LTD
TAIWAN STOCK EXCHANGE
PRICE CHANGE: TWD +0.60
OPEN: TWD 58.30   CLOSE: TWD 58.90

We should likewise let the photographer Edward Burtynsky take us to China and show us the sacrifice behind many of the wondrously cheap goods we are delighted to buy: the irons, coffee makers, barbecue grills, citrus juicers, vacuum cleaners and toasters that are turned out in prodigious numbers by Tsann Kuen Enterprise in a hangar-like 23,000-person factory in Xiamen City in south-east China.

We should remember that these items are – of course – very cheap not because Tsann Kuen Enterprise is so wondrous or clever and modern technology so ingenious, but principally because workers around Xiamen City suffer grievously from a condition that economists would politely call 'a lack of pricing power' – and we might more frankly identify as desperation.

THALES SA
PARIS STOCK EXCHANGE
PRICE CHANGE: EUR +0.08
OPEN: EUR 27.00   CLOSE: EUR 27.08

Yet this shouldn't prevent moments when we can also admire the beauty of production, like that found in the Pléiades-HR 1A earth-observation satellite, as it reveals its innards in the assembly halls of the Thales factory in Cannes, France. Our wicked species is rarely more impressive than when it is quietly engaged in a complex,

Benedict Redgrove, *Satellite Manufacture, Cannes*, 2010.

ordered task. Given our capacity for indolence and chaos, it can be moving to contemplate the sheer precision, exactitude and discipline that most work demands. Like watching a person sleep, it is hard not to feel an a priori benevolence towards someone whom one has observed adroitly wiring up a satellite.

AMCOR LTD
AUSTRALIAN STOCK EXCHANGE
PRICE CHANGE: $ -0.11
OPEN: $ 8.30   CLOSE: $ 8.19

We should in addition be prompted to give some thought to the *meaning* of our frenzied labours. Most of us won't, of course, ever have heard of Amcor, one of Australia's most profitable companies and the world's largest maker of tissue cartons, nappy boxes, toothpaste dispensers, suncream tubes and shampoo bottles, but the great fortunes of our day have rarely been accumulated through the sale of the most meaningful items and services, such as poetry or relationship counselling.

When does a job feel meaningful? When we can, at the end of the day, feel as if our work has in some way, however modestly, helped either to reduce the misery or to increase the contentment of others. We like to serve, and we like even more to experience the impact of our efforts on the lives of our fellow humans. Yet when labour is subdivided into ever smaller parts, when whole careers are devoted to turning out objects which will affect another's well-being for only a second or not at all, then meaning suffers. Not that the stock markets would care; they would reply that meaning should be something reserved for the weekend.

Stock indices leave one juggling a set of varied feelings: an admiration for the fertility of modern business, a wonder at the extraordinary degree of intelligence and effort demanded to suceed in any industry, and yet a guilty sense of the absurdity and waste of so much of our toil and, in the middle of the night, when the mind tends to avenge itself on the compromises of the day, a pained wonder at what we might be doing with the ever-more precious bit that still remains of our lives.

SAP AG
FRANKFURT STOCK EXCHANGE
PRICE CHANGE: EUR -0.10
OPEN: EUR 59.70   CLOSE: EUR 59.60

We can conclude that the numbers and graphs in financial news are only ever a shorthand for the stories and images that we need in order to understand the world we have built. Business is ultimately too interesting and too significant to be described only for the sake of those who want to invest in it.

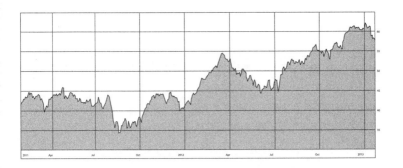

A sweeping story that needs a modern Emile Zola to tell it:
the software manufacturer SAP's share price, 2011–13.

v.

Celebrity

Admiration

Interviewer: Usain Bolt is, hands down, the fastest person on the planet ... There's no one else quite like the Golden Bolt ... You are my hero. So how does that make you feel?

Bolt: I feel good.

Interviewer: How do you feel? When you get down on those blocks and you're about to explode, what actually goes through the Golden Bolt's mind?

Bolt: All you try to do is just relax, really. For me, it's always just trying to compose myself, try to not think about anything, because as soon as something comes into your mind, then you are going to be in a lot of trouble.

Interviewer: What does it take to be a champion, not just any old champion, [but] to be a great champion?

Bolt: Well, it's just hard work ... Just hard work and dedication.

Interviewer: What is it that motivates you most now? Is it the winning? Is it being the champ? Is it money? Is it fame? Is it the women?

Bolt: It's everything.

Interviewer: How many times have you been properly in love in your life? ¶

CNN

1.

THE NEWS CONSTANTLY introduces us to a parade of extraordinary men and women: people who can run faster than anyone else on earth, who know how to make us laugh, who have started revolutionary businesses, who can design succulent meals and whose faces are flawlessly beautiful. Their achievements, personalities and good looks excite us as few other things can. As a result, we often want to ask them how they did it, hear them talk about their childhoods, observe what they are wearing, find out whom they are in love with, peek inside their homes, follow them to the seaside and even accompany them across the road when they go out to buy groceries.

2.

THIS SORT OF interest is almost universally condemned by the guardians of elite culture; in serious company, it isn't generally endearing to reveal a devotion to celebrity news. Partly this comes down to the belief, widely shared among elites, that celebrities can't reasonably be deemed admirable or worthy subjects of interest when their contributions to society are held up against the backdrop of humanity's true problems. In the rare case where the merit of a public figure's achievement is indisputable, the high-minded suggestion is that we should focus exclusively on the actual accomplishment (the business started or the film made) rather than fixate on its author – as we are wont to do, often, to the point where we become obsessed by the smallest details of his or her life, such as whom he took with him to a dinner party or how she tied her hair

Emma Watson buys strawberries,
New York City, 2012 (Splash News).

back at the beach. The elite implication is that there is something demeaning and childish about the need to hero-worship a famous person who is our contemporary but who doesn't know us: it seems passive and inferior, a confession of inadequacy, a proof that we are insufficiently engaged with our own projects and ambitions and have chosen to 'escape' from our lives because we have no idea how to lead them properly.

3.

THIS IS A pity – and rather problematic too, for if serious people judge the very concept of celebrity to be beneath them, then the role of anointing celebrities will fall to organizations entirely untroubled by the prospect of appealing to the lowest appetites.

Furthermore, without proper consideration of the purpose of celebrity, we will find it difficult to think through what we might sensibly want from the famous people who live among us. Can admiration lead anywhere worthwhile? Is there anything substantial or important to be gained from revering others?

4.

THE IMPULSE TO admire is an ineradicable and important feature of our psyches. Ignoring or condemning it won't kill it off; it will simply force it underground, where it will lurk untended and undeveloped, prone to latch on to inappropriate targets. Rather than try to suppress our love of celebrity, we ought to channel it in optimally intelligent and fruitful directions. A properly organized

Bravery
Heracles of Mantinea,
c. 460 BC.

Athletic Prowess
Unknown athlete throwing a discus,
460–450 BC.

Leadership
Pericles, 430 BC.

society would be one where the best-known people were those who embodied and reinforced the highest, noblest and most socially beneficial values, and hence one in which an admission of reverence for a given celebrity would be an occasion for pride rather than a prompt for shame or self-deprecating laughter.

5.

IN ITS GOLDEN age, the ancient city-state of Athens was unembarrassed about the act of admiration. The city held a number of virtues dear. It believed in democratic government, military valour, intellectual freedom, civic glory, artistic expression and athleticism. However, its belief in these qualities wasn't abstract; it focused on a range of exceptional people who realized them in concentrated form – and who found themselves, as a result, celebrated and commemorated in statues, festivals and works of literature. Statesmen like Pericles and Demosthenes, athletes like Philammon the Olympic boxer and Chabrias the chariot racer and musicians like Melanippides and Anakreon were looked up to as practical guides to a life of εὐδαιμονία (*eudaimonia*) or 'flourishing'.

In its own history, Catholicism has similarly commended to its believers a cohort of worthy individuals in the hope that their example will provoke admiration and emulation: some 10,000 saints whose good character and deeds are meant to reflect the central Christian virtues of humility, liberality, chastity, gentleness, temperance, patience and diligence. In compendia of lives of the saints, such as the late-medieval bestseller *The Golden Legend*, everything about these canonized men and women was held to be

The finger of St Catherine of Siena in a silver reliquary.

Patron Saint of Difficult Marriages
St Gengulphus of Burgundy.

Patron Saint of Failures
St Birgitta of Sweden.

significant and deserving of attention: what sorts of foods they liked, what clothes they wore, who their families were, what colour their hair was. Furthermore, it didn't strike medieval Christianity as unseemly, after these saints had been dead for a time, to disinter them, cut their skeletons up and put bits of their bones in special niches and chapels, to which one was invited to travel often great distances in order to worship and take inspiration.

What underlies both the Christian and the Athenian approaches to celebrity is a commitment to the idea of self-improvement, as well as the belief that it is via immersion in the lives of great exemplars that we stand the richest chance of learning how to become better versions of ourselves. Catholicism specifically advises us that at problematic moments in our lives, we ought to ask what a given saint would do in our place. During a domestic argument, we should, for example, think of the calm and forgiving nature of St Gengulphus of Burgundy, the patron saint of difficult marriages, or equally, when facing professional humiliation, we might regain our composure by summoning an image of the unparanoid and gentle St Birgitta of Sweden, the patron saint of failures.

6.

THE APPROACH OF the Catholic Church towards its saints and that of the ancient Athenians towards their orators and discus throwers provides important clues as to how we ourselves might best negotiate modern celebrity.

A first lesson is that we should endeavour to become a little clearer about what it is that we actually find interesting in the characters we admire. The news seldom helps us here, for it tends to leave the deeper sources of curiosity about celebrities untapped and so prevents us from using their examples properly. It simply circles around famous people with a kind of manic energy, asking them again and again what a certain achievement 'felt like', or posing a succession of bland logistical queries about when their new film will start shooting or else positioning tenacious paparazzi in the bushes to capture their expressions as they leave the dry cleaner's – as though these tactics could really assuage the inner itch generated by something good which one evidently detects in a confused way within a celebrity's personality.

Keeping the example of the Catholics in mind, we should try to locate those celebrities who can best function as guides to virtues we need to bolster in ourselves, perhaps bravery or playfulness, wisdom or creativity, confidence or forgiveness. Out of the hundreds of celebrities that the news introduces us to (from peace negotiators to painters, sports stars to neuroscientists), we should pick out for ourselves a set of people of genuine worth, whose attitudes and achievements can inspire us to lead more successful and contented lives. With no supernatural intent or childish idealism, we can be fortified by holding in our minds a loose ensemble of secular 'patron saints', famous people to whom our thoughts may turn for encouragement and inspiration at moments of sterility and lassitude.

To help in this quest to use celebrities more productively, we should redesign that grievously flawed staple of the news: the celebrity interview. A genre at present predominantly fixated on personal revelations and undirected questions about 'the new project', the interview should in the future become a chance to answer one question above all others: 'What can we learn from this famous person?' It shouldn't matter that the celebrity operates in a field different from our own. Lessons are transferable and virtues operative across activities. The ideal celebrity interview would help us to answer such questions as: 'Although I am not a tennis player, what can I learn from the attitude to a bad call displayed in the second set by the eventual Wimbledon winner?' Or: 'Although I have no artistic ambitions, how might the example of the multi-talented artist, adept at everything from pottery to architecture, breathe energy into my own career plans?'

We should cease to treat the better celebrities like magical apparitions fit only for passive wonder or sneaky curiosity. They are ordinary humans who have achieved extraordinary feats through hard work and strategic thinking. We should treat them as case studies to be pored over and rigorously dissected with a basic question in mind: 'What can I absorb from this person?' The interest that currently latches on to details of celebrities' clothes or diet should be channelled towards a project of growth. In the ideal news service of the future, every celebrity story would at heart be a piece of education: an invitation to learn from an admirable person about how to become a slightly better version of oneself.

7.

WE ARE USED to thinking that anyone who 'copies' a celebrity is sad and inauthentic, but in its highest form, imitation founded on admiration is integral to a good life. To refuse to admire, to take no interest in what distinguished others are up to, is to shut ourselves off, grandly and implausibly, from important knowledge.

The job of the news is to make the celebrity section no less exciting than it is now, while ensuring that it provides us with psychologically rich, pedagogic portraits of certain noble-minded individuals who will spark our imaginations because they properly help us to address the flaws in our personalities and the knots in our ambitions. Celebrity news should, in its mature form, be a serious and respectable medium through which we learn to become more than we currently are.

Envy

For a rich guy with a private jet and a million-dollar sports car, Elon Musk is unusually quiet and shy. He is tall, with long arms and big hands and a boyish face that often looks distracted; you can tell the wheels inside his head never quite stop spinning. Before he founded SpaceX in 2002, Musk created two Internet companies: Zip2, which he sold to Compaq in 1999 for $307 million in cash, and PayPal, which went public shortly before being sold to eBay. Musk, the largest shareholder, was 30 years old. ¶

Wired

1.

THE WEEKEND CAN be the time for the softer bits of news: the colour supplements, the tech, design and media blogs, the style sections and the interview and profile pieces. This is where we may learn, over the course of an hour or so of browsing, about the twenty-five-year-old chef who runs four successful seafood restaurants in Lower Manhattan, about the fashion label started up by the daughter of a well-known film director, about the Silicon Valley entrepreneur who has set up an online university backed by $1 billion in Qatari venture capital money, about the revered German artist at work on his own museum in Berlin and about the former Wall Street banker who is about to open twenty boutique hotels across China – all of this on a morning that began with a sense of inner ease, calm and dedication to domestic goals, with the sun filtering through the curtains and the sound of birds in the garden outside.

2.

WE LIVE IN an age unlike any other in the extent to which it foregrounds the idea of individual opportunity. For most of history, we lived and died on the same rung of the social ladder. Our parents' occupations determined our own. Prospects for betterment did not exist. Financial markets were primitive and capital not easily available. Technological discoveries came along every 200 years, and political change even less frequently.

Now, as the news attests with its constant stories of initiative, perseverance, toil and self-realization, there are theoretically no limits to what anyone can achieve. Everything is – allegedly – possible for the creative and the tenacious. Right now, across the continents, the cleverest ones among us are finding ingenious ways to raise money, draft scripts, invent formulae and design machines that will change the fundamentals of existence. A contented resignation to a modest condition has come to seem not only a grave error, but possibly a sign of mental illness.

In response to the stories of achievement it places before us, the news invites us to feel content and mature: quietly pleased by the tycoon's success, impressed by the entrepreneur's initiative, thoughtfully interested in the artist's global fame. News organizations that otherwise warn us of the damaging side effects of strobe lighting, nudity or profane language see no need to prepare us for the potentially problematic consequences of witnessing the success of others. They expect us to be grateful for the haphazard selection of victors that they have, this week like all others, worked so hard to parade before us. They imply that we might sit around the kitchen table on a Saturday morning good-naturedly taking in information about these titans without registering any particularly harmful or troubling after-thoughts, simply a broad sense of delight at the sheer genius and resourcefulness of mankind.

3.

BUT INSTEAD, DEEP down, some of us are likely to be caving in under the pressure of envy, feeling the ache of our tragically ignored and soon-to-be-forgotten egos in a world of apparently infinite possibility. Beneath an impassive surface, we may be in agony over the contrast between the hopes that were once invested in us and the reality of what we have done with our lives, the difference between what others our own age (and even some much younger) have shown themselves capable of achieving and the trivial accomplishments to which our hesitant, timid and directionless selves can lay claim. While this might be cause enough for some moments of touching melancholy, after a certain point even self-pity ceases to be interesting.

Existential panic may not, of course, seem like the most reasonable reaction to an upbeat, glossily illustrated feature entitled 'Silicon Valley's Top Twenty Investors', but after scanning such a story, we may nevertheless come perilously close to hurling the supplement to one side, banging our fists on the table and, with an anguished sob, screaming at a world that doesn't care (or at our surprised spouse, in the act of preparing lunch), *'I can't take being me any more!'*

4.

THE NEWS SHOULD help us with our feelings. It shouldn't pretend that it is normal to present an audience with repeated evidence of the accomplishments of the most energetic and inventive members of the species and not expect that people will be driven a little crazy as a result. It should admit that it takes an exceptionally unimaginative person to read of someone of their own age and gender who has bought and sold businesses, consorted with the mighty and attracted the attention of millions – and in response, experience only a broad and serene pleasure. It should be generous enough to recognize that we urgently need help in understanding, interpreting and living with the envy it so regularly unleashes upon its unsuspecting and undefended consumers.

5.

WHILE ENVY HAS always been a target of fierce and moralistic criticism, it is also an indispensable feature of a decent life. It is a call to action that should be heeded, for it contains garbled messages sent by muddled but important parts of our personalities about what we should be doing with the rest of our lives. Listening to envy should help us to take painful yet necessary steps towards becoming who we really are.

Instead of trying to repress our envy, we should therefore make every effort to study it. Each person we envy possesses some piece of the jigsaw puzzle depicting our possible future condition. There is a portrait of our 'true self' waiting to be assembled out of the envious hints we receive when we flick through a magazine, turn the pages of a newspaper or hear updates on the radio about the latest career moves of our old schoolmates. Though we might at first experience envy as humiliating and a confirmation of our own failure, we should calmly ask one essential and redemptive question of all those we envy: 'What could I learn here?' It is a pity that envious reactions are so often confusingly vague and accompanied by panic. We start to envy certain individuals in their entirety, when in fact, if we took a moment to analyse their lives calmly, we would realize that it is only a small part of what they have done that really resonates with, and should guide, our own next steps.

6.

WE NEVER ENVY another's achievement more than when we know very little about how it was attained. If news organizations were kinder, rather than simply describing the triumphs of others as mysterious faits accomplis, they would expend copious energy on analysing precisely what went into them. They would present the stories of successful people principally as case studies that we could understand and practically emulate rather than simply, as at present, either admire blankly or resent.

7.

THERE ARE OF course limits to the uses of envy. Too many random reminders of other people's success may simply terrify us into inactivity and unwittingly prevent us from putting any single plan into practice. In order to achieve anything on our own, we need to be free for extended stretches from the psychological pressures exerted by news of others' feats. We require periods of inner seclusion and calm if we are ever going to finish off something worthwhile: that is, something that we may ourselves one day be envied for.

The news should also help us by reminding us of statistical realities. While the supplements may be continuously filled with success stories, success itself will always remain highly anomalous, achieved by no more than a few thousand out of many millions – a detail that the editors of the news carefully (and sadistically) keep carefully out of our imaginations.

In contrast to what the news suggests, most businesses in fact fail, most films don't get made, most careers are not stellar, most people's faces and bodies are less than perfectly beautiful and almost everyone is sad and worried a lot of the time. We shouldn't lament our own condition just because it doesn't measure up against a deeply unrealistic benchmark, or hate ourselves solely for our inability to defy some breathtaking odds.

After we've explored envy as thoroughly as we can, we should be offered a chance to feel collectively distraught over, rather than individually persecuted for, how little we have been able to achieve.

The Will to Fame

The World's Most Powerful Celebrities:

70.   Dwayne Johnson, $36 million
71.   Maria Sharapova, $26 million
72.   Ben Stiller, $33 million
73.   Khloe Kardashian Odom, $11 million
74.   Seth MacFarlane, $36 million
75.   Charlize Theron, $18 million
76.   Sofia Vergara, $19 million
77.   Serena Williams, $13 million
78.   Alec Baldwin, $15 million
79.   Janet Evanovich, $33 million ¶

Forbes

1.

WHY DO PEOPLE want to become famous? It's easy enough to mock celebrities, but where in the psyche does the will to fame spring from? Few of us ever become famous by accident or at little cost, so what is it that inspires the deep sacrifices that fame demands?

2.

AT THE HEART of the desire for fame lies a touching, vulnerable and simple aspiration: a longing to be treated *nicely*. Whatever secondary impetus may be supplied by appetites for money, luxury, sex or power, it is really the wish for respect that drives the will to fame.

If this hardly seems like a fuel powerful enough to propel a lifetime's worth of the efforts that becoming and remaining famous require, we should never underestimate the negative stimulus provided by fame's opposite, humiliation. We may come to want fame desperately because of just how searing is the pain of being overlooked, patronized, left alone in the corner, ordered to go to the end of the line, thought of as a nobody or told to call back in a few weeks. The wish to be famous is a bid to have our dignity fully respected in a world where it almost certainly won't be unless we are prepared to take extreme measures. We may be equal before the law and at the ballot box, but there is no guarantee of dignity in the treatment we receive at the office, in our social life or between the wheels of governmental or commercial bureaucracies. Especially in big cities, those centres of unkindness towards the ordinary, where life is unmediated by the beneficial influence of vast skies and huge horizons, respect is a scarce and tightly rationed commodity, and indifference is the norm. One would be well advised not to set foot in Manhattan or Los Angeles without having at the ready a fairly snappy and impressive answer to the inevitable enquiry about what one does for a living.

3.

FAME ALLOWS CELEBRITIES to leverage kindness and respect from others. A famous name alone can accomplish in an instant what its bearer might otherwise have had to beg for over years with his or her whole personality. This saves a lot of time.

Other people have to be nice to the famous because they appear as emanations of the whole world, of the judgement of millions of their followers. Fame is power backed up by an unseen army of admirers. To refuse to laugh at a celebrity's joke, or to express scepticism as to their talent, is to take on not just an individual but also the whole system that anointed them: the clever judges who gave them the prize, the legions of people who bought their album, the venerable magazines which put them on their covers, all of these are part of an invisible but highly effective force which the famous person can command whenever he or she meets someone at a party or has to deal with an official at a check-in desk. Fame staves off tendencies towards opportunistic meanness; it saves the famous person from being left at the mercy of strangers.

4.

BUT NOT EVERYONE needs fame equally badly. The appetite for fame tends to depend on both what sort of childhood one had and what sort of society one lives in.

In the early years of the archetypal famous person, there is – almost inevitably – rejection; there can't be any kind of sustained longing for fame without it. One parent or other had to have been uninterested, emotionally absent, more concerned with a sibling – or dead. In the most desperate cases, where there is no question but that fame will become an obsession, the parent omitted to notice their own child because they were themselves engaged in trying to become, or in consorting with those who already were, famous.

When attention and kindness most mattered, when they were defenceless and weak between the ages of zero and ten, when they had no sophisticated tools for attracting the love of others beyond their mere existence, the embryonically famous could not spontaneously convince a much-needed parent of their own importance, a slight catastrophic enough to shape the trajectory of an entire life. How invisible one was once made to feel determines how special and omnipresent one will later need to be.

Unfortunately, of course, achieving fame rarely corrects the early slight, for the real wish is not to impress through achievement (singing, sculpting, deal making and so on), but to be loved simply for *being*. The moment of achieving fame is hence likely to be accompanied by feelings of hollowness, for it can't in itself correct the humiliation that ignited the original wish for fame. The self-destructive behaviour often seen in the famous is the confused articulation of anger at a pyrrhic victory, a desire to destroy an adulation of the many which has been unable to compensate for the neglect of a primary crucial few.

By contrast, the happily anonymous adult, who needs no acclaim and can be satisfied with a modest job, is the true person of privilege in this scenario, for he or she has luxuriated in one of the greatest gifts available to man: the sense of being central in the affections and care of a parental figure. A decade of parental love can give a person strength enough to cope with fifty years of insignificance. The only childhood properly deserving of the epithet 'privileged' is one in which the child's emotional needs were adequately met.

This analysis has a side benefit of providing us with a litmus test for how good a job we may be doing parenting our own children: we have only to ask whether they have any wish whatsoever to become famous.

5.

THE INTENSITY OF the desire for fame depends also on the nature of one's society. The more dignity and kindness are given only to the very few, the stronger will be the urge to avoid being simply normal. Those who pin the blame for 'celebrity culture' at the door of the immoral young are hence missing the point. The real cause of celebrity culture isn't narcissistic shallowness, it is a deficit of kindness. A society where everyone wants to be famous is also one where, for a variety of essentially political (in the broad sense) reasons, being ordinary has failed to deliver the degree of respect necessary to satisfy people's natural appetite for dignity.

In so far as the modern world is celebrity-obsessed, we are living not so much in superficial times as in unkind ones. Fame has become a means to an end, the most direct route to a kind of respect that could otherwise have been won in different, less renown-dependent ways – through kindness rather than magazine covers.

If we want to decrease the urge for fame, we should not begin by frowning upon or seeking to censor news about celebrities; we should start to think of ways of making kindness, patience and attention more widely available, especially to the young.

The Injuries of Fame

The High Court in London has just ruled that a column satirizing Elton John was not defamatory. Elton John had claimed that the article in the *Guardian* made fun of his serious charity work. He claimed it even joked about important events, such as the White Tie Ball, saying he only held them for self-promotion and to meet celebrities, not to raise money ... Elton John described the article as having a 'gratuitously offensive, nasty and snide tone'. However, the judge disagreed, saying, 'The words complained of ... could not be understood by a reasonable reader of the Guardian Weekend section as containing the serious allegation pleaded.' Elton John was seeking damages and an apology. In a statement, Guardian News & Media said, 'We're sorry that Elton John lost his sense of humour over this article ... Newspapers have published satire since the 17th century in this country: the judgment is an important recognition of the right to poke the occasional bit of fun.' ❡

Perezhilton.com

I.

THOSE SETTING OUT to be famous dream of securing a particular kind of attention for themselves: *high-grade attention*, by which they imagine an audience sympathetic to their talents and forgiving of their faults, an audience that resembles a loving parent, an ideal teacher or an all-seeing and generous God.

Then, once famous, they realize that they have become the recipient of a most perplexing kind of attention: one where intense love is followed by sudden hatred, where their most minor lapses are treated with violent intolerance, where weaknesses are pounced upon and never forgotten, where a prurient interest surrounds matters entirely unrelated to the talent that initially earned them public notice, where journalists go through their rubbish in the early hours and where embarrassing pictures of them appear online and within hours attract the ridicule of millions. If they were to complain about this kind of attention, what might be termed *low-grade attention*, they would quickly and sanctimoniously be put in their place and informed that someone who courts attention cannot choose which version they are accorded and must be ready for, and even deserve, any sort of attention whatsoever.

2.

CELEBRITIES ARE SO unusual and so privileged that it takes a little effort to remember that they aren't a different species in every respect and indeed that they are especially like you and me in one area in particular: they get hurt very easily.

The exaggerated need for approval that drove them to be famous in the first place makes them particularly unprepared for coping with the taunts and denigration they can be sure to face once they have a name. They will be forced to understand that their reputation is not theirs alone, but is a co-creation between themselves and their audiences over which they have appallingly imperfect and indirect control. Shepherding a reputation has some of the futility of trying to guide a soap bubble. When insult strikes, inside their frightened minds everyone has read the venomous articles and seen the embarrassing pictures and will believe the worst. The fears about themselves that made the celebrities struggle to win fame have turned out to be real: they truly are the monsters they tried to persuade themselves and the world that they were not.

3.

A STANCE OF heroic defiance is sometimes suggested at this point; the wounded celebrity is advised to be the bearer of his or her own meaning and to disregard what the world is saying. But how could anyone become famous without a disposition to care a little too much about what other people think?

A better tactic would be to get into the minds of one's enemies. The famous person might imagine their critics to be motivated solely by a limitless, obsessive hatred, and to have made their lacerating deductions from immovable convictions. But in truth, their opponents are generally not much more than thoughtless, unempathetic, inured to low standards and accustomed to doing what others do. Their cruel jibes arise chiefly from the sheer implausibility that the person they are being mean to could actually be listening and is likely to be deeply vulnerable. As when one is dropping a bomb from high altitude, the capacity for hurting others increases hugely when one doesn't have to look one's victim in the eye.

4.

THE REASONS WHY we need others to fail and why we delight in gossip about their missteps are in the end deeply sad; because we are furious about our own lack of attention – and so attempt to gain relief by punishing those who seem to have deprived us of our due. Our disappointed ambitions turn us into failures: people who need others to fail.

The urge to gossip and the desire for fame spring from the very same ill: both are caused by a shortage of attention. Celebrities are really only trying – albeit on a much larger stage and scale – to solve the same problem we all grapple with, that of being ignored. We might even say that famous people stand in relation to failures of attention much as the fearless pioneers of flight stood in relation to air travel. Although many of these early airmen died in violent explosions and crashes, the ultimate goal was that one day everyone might be able to fly safely, just as the hope in the arena of fame is that dignity will over time grow more common, and that the sort of respect that is now still the preserve of only a few will some day become properly and democratically prevalent.

We are still working out what the word *democracy* really signifies. At first, it reflected a conviction that power shouldn't just be in the hands of the few. It took a great deal of time, sensitization and political articulation for this point to get across and for elites to recognize that being deprived of the right to vote deserved to be listed among the very real ills that a ruler might inflict on his or her people. We should now move the democratic process along and accept that we have other needs which are no less urgent or important than the need to vote, among which we must include the need for dignity and respect. We should sensitize ourselves to the immense psychological repercussions of being pushed around and humiliated. A society which routinely debases the greatest share of its members will find itself afflicted by a strong desire for fame, mixed in with eruptions of the most sarcastic, vindictive and schizophrenic attacks on the few who have managed to secure renown.

The solution to both vicious gossip and the overardent longing for fame lies in a manoeuvre all but unimaginable within the current arrangement of society: a broader distribution of high-grade attention. With more of this in circulation, the manic need both to insult the few and to stand out from the many would abate, to the flourishing of all.

VI.

Disaster

Tragedy

A Manhattan doctor plunged 30 stories to his death from his Upper East Side high-rise yesterday in an apparent suicide, police and witnesses said. The body of Dr. Sheldon 'Shelly' Steinbach, 68, an anesthesiologist, slammed into a second-floor balcony at the building, at 246 E. 63rd St., at 9:35 a.m. 'I heard a large bang, and we looked outside and saw him. His body just exploded,' said resident Jonathan Kershner, 25, who lives two floors above where the doctor landed. 'Then a doorman came by saying a woman was looking for her husband,' Kershner added. Steinbach had a Twitter page but had not updated it since October 2011. The personal description on his account reads: 'I am an anesthesiologist in New York City and am having a great day. Married. Love aerobic activities and music.' ¶

New York Post

1.

EVERY TIME WE connect with the news, we can be sure that we will be confronted by graphic accounts of some of the most appalling eventualities that can befall our species: a depressed man leaps out of the window, a mother poisons her children, a teacher rapes his pupil, a husband beheads his wife, a teenager shoots his classmates. The news leads us very reliably into the crucible of human horror.

A decent impulse is to look away and to insist that such deaths and traumas are simply too sad and too private to be subjected to a stranger's gaze. Any curiosity seems, from this perspective, to be a particularly shameful and modern kind of pathology.

Motivated by fears of intrusion, the more serious news organizations typically adopt a reserved tone in their reports on the sorts of events that severely test any faith one might still have in the reasonableness and decency of mankind.

They leave it to their less dignified colleagues, unfettered by scruples, to evoke the truly vivid details of the latest outrages: to give us a close-up view of the body after it fell from the balcony, the bedroom where the little child was tied up or the carving knife with the spouse's blood still on its blade. Their reward for being willing to undertake such investigations is the occasionally guilty but concerted and lucrative interest of many millions of readers and viewers.

2.

IT ISN'T HARD to characterize the interest of the public in horror stories as tasteless and unproductive. But beneath the surface banality, we should allow that we are often – in confused and inarticulate ways – attempting to get at something important. When immersing ourselves in blood-soaked narratives, we are not always solely in search of entertainment or distraction; we are not always being merely prurient or callously appropriating intensities of feeling that our own lives have failed to provide.

We may also be looking to expose ourselves to barbaric tales to help us retain a tighter hold on our more civilized selves – and in particular, to nurture our always ephemeral reserves of patience, self-control, forgiveness and empathy.

Rather than just inveigh moralistically against our fascination with heinous events, the challenge should be to tweak how they are reported – in order that they better release their important, yet too often latent, emotional and societal benefits.

3.

EVERY YEAR, AT the end of March, the citizens of ancient Athens would gather under open skies on the southern slopes of the Acropolis in the Theatre of Dionysus and there listen to the latest works by the great tragedians of their city. The plot lines of these plays were unmitigatingly macabre, easily matching anything our own news could provide: a man kills his father, marries his mother and gouges out his own eyes (*Oedipus Rex*); a man has his daughter murdered as part of a plan to revenge the infidelity of his brother's wife (*Iphigenia*); a mother murders her two children to spoil her unfaithful husband's plans to start a new family with another woman (*Medea*).

Rather than regarding these stories as grotesque spectacles that all right-minded people should avoid, in his *Poetics* of c. 335 BC, the philosopher Aristotle looked generously upon the human fascination with them. He proposed that, when they are well written and artfully staged, such stories can become crucial resources for the emotional and moral education of a whole society. Despite the barbarity they describe, they themselves can function as civilizing forces.

But in order for this to happen, in order for a *horror* (a meaningless narration of revolting events) to turn into what Aristotle called a *tragedy* (an educative tale fashioned from abominations), the philosopher thought it was vital that the plot should be well arranged and the motives and the personalities of the characters properly outlined to us. Extreme dramatic skill would be required in order for the audience to spontaneously reach a point at which it recognized that the apparently unhinged protagonist of the story, who had acted impetuously, arrogantly and blindly, who had perhaps killed others and destroyed his own reputation and life, the person whom one might at first (had one come across the story in the news) dismissed as nothing but a maniac, was, in the final analysis, rather like us in certain key ways. A work of tragedy would rise to its true moral and edifying possibilities when the audience looked upon the hero's ghastly errors and crimes and was left with no option but to reach the terrifying conclusion: 'How easily I, too, might have done the same.' Tragedy's task was to demonstrate the ease with which an essentially decent and likeable person could end up generating hell.

If we were entirely sane, if madness did not have a serious grip on one side of us, other people's tragedies would hold a great deal less interest for us. While we circle gruesome stories in the

A man drives into his family home to punish his wife, Manchester, 2012.

Medea kills her son to punish her husband, Greek jar, c. 330 BC.

Our fascination with crimes may be part of an unconscious effort
to make sure we never commit them.

media, we may at a highly unconscious level be exploring shocking but important questions: 'If things got really out of hand late one night, and I was feeling wound up and tired and insecure, might I be capable of killing my partner?' 'If I was divorced and my spouse was keeping my children from me, would I ever be able to kill them in a form of twisted revenge?' 'Could I ever start chatting with a minor on the Internet and, without quite realizing the enormity of what I was doing, end up trying to seduce him or her?'

For civilization to proceed, we naturally need the answers to be a firm *no* in all cases. There is a serious task for the news here: the disasters we are introduced to should be framed in order to give us the maximum encouragement to practise *not* doing the things that the more chaotic parts of us would – under extreme circumstances – be attracted to exploring. We may never actually fling our children off a bridge at the end of our access day or shoot our partner dead during an argument, but we are all, at times, emotionally in the space where these sorts of things can happen. Tragedies remind us how badly we need to keep controlling ourselves by showing us what happens when people don't.

4.

TRAGEDIES SHOULDN'T ONLY help us to be good, they should also prompt us to be kind. How likely we are to be sympathetic to someone who kills their spouse or children depends in large part on how their story happens to be told to us: what information we are given about them, how we are introduced to their motives and with what degree of insight and complexity their psyches are laid before us.

In Greek tragedies, a Chorus regularly interrupts events to direct sentiments and richly contextualize characters' actions. It tends to speak with solemn respect about the protagonists, whatever the sins they have committed. Such sensitivity ensures that few audience members are likely to leave a performance of *Oedipus Rex* dismissing the unfortunate central character as a 'loser' or 'psycho'.

The news is less careful in its narrations; and our judgements are – as a result – far more intemperate and nastier.

> A Teesside doctor who downloaded more than 1,300 child porn images, including scenes of torture, has been jailed. Police found the 'sickening' images on the laptop of James Taylor, 31, from Wensleydale Gardens, Thornaby. The doctor, who worked at Pinderfields Hospital in Wakefield, earlier admitted looking at indecent images of children. Taylor was sentenced to a year and a day in prison by a judge at Teesside Crown Court on Friday and was banned from working with children for life. ¶
>
> **BBC**

At first glance, the doctor seems to deserve no sympathy whatsoever. But our decision about how we consider him is crucially dependent on how the facts of his case are presented to us. We could sympathize with more or less anyone if their story was told to us in a certain way – *and we wouldn't necessarily be wrong to do so* (as Dostoevsky or Jesus would have reminded us).

In the context of news reporting, this claim seems contentious, even dangerous, because we have to juggle two ideas which sound opposing: that we can sympathize with a criminal and at the same time firmly condemn his or her crime. The news is tacitly convinced that its audience wouldn't be able to pull off this conceptual feat, and that any sympathy it might express would lead the audience to want to open up the prisons and let murderers roam the streets. It hence remains steadfast in its refusal to undertake the narrative and psychological manoeuvres required to humanize criminals.

Instead it rushes through their stories. A performance of *Oedipus Rex* might last an hour and a half; the news story in which the doctor appears is 304 words long.

Inevitably, a feeling of outrage is likely to be at its height when we confront the headline:

Doctor had 'sickening' child porn

But, as we read on, our certainty might be challenged. Towards the end of the piece, we learn:

> Ordering Taylor to sign the Sex Offenders Register for 10 years, the judge said: 'As a result of this conviction no doubt your career will come to an end.'

We might feel a chill at the thought of how seven long years of medical school had come to this. The article gives a hint of the panic the doctor must have felt:

> The court was told Taylor initially denied being responsible, but later admitted, during police interviews, that he had downloaded the images.

And the enormous price that he has subsequently had to pay:

> Stephen Rich, defending, told Judge George Moor-
> house that Taylor's wife and newborn baby had left him
> and that his life had collapsed. ¶

An addendum informs us that while in prison, the man tried to commit suicide. All this is no less sad than the plot line of *Madame Bovary* or *Hamlet* – and, let's argue, the character of the doctor is not fundamentally any worse; Hamlet is, after all, a murderer and Emma Bovary is guilty of extreme child cruelty. We consider them 'tragic' figures – that is, entitled to a degree of complex understanding – because we imagine that there must have been something unusually noble and dignified about their nature and circumstances. But really it is only the generosity of spirit of Flaubert and Shakespeare that elevates Bovary and Hamlet above the ordinary criminal and dissuades us from judging them as harshly as we might the imprisoned doctor.

5.

WHEN REPORTING ON a tragedy, the news tends to make dreadful conduct seem unique to a particular person. It resists the wider resonance and the more helpful conclusion: that we are all a hair's breadth away from catastrophe. This knowledge should, if properly absorbed, sink us into a mood of reflective, mature sadness. We are more implicated than we might like to believe in the misdeeds of other members of our species. A lack of a serious criminal record is in large measure a matter of luck and good circumstance, not proof of an incorruptible nature. A clean conscience is the preserve of those without sufficient imagination. Were life, or what the Greeks termed the gods, ever really to test us, we would almost surely be found wanting – an awareness upon which a measure of understanding towards the guilty should be founded.

The tragedians of ancient Greece never forgot this. They liked to tell us how vicious, stupid, sexual, enraged and blind we could be, but they allowed room for complex compassion as well. Through the examples they leave us, we are coaxed into accepting that we are members of a noble but hideously flawed species; capable of performing amazing feats, ably practising medicine or parenting with love for many years, and then of turning around and blowing up our existence with a single rash move. We should be scared.

6.

THE ANCIENT GREEKS saw tragic plays once a year, at a specific time, within a particular context and with some knowledge of the works' larger purpose.

By contrast, we take in tragic news stories almost every day, but we rarely recognize them as belonging to a coherent narrative cycle with a distinctive moral to impart. The news doesn't help us to place in a single genre all those incidents in which self-control is lost and the monster within is released. It doesn't, as it should, gather all its varied tales of horror under the unified heading of 'Tragedy' and then narrate them in such a way that we can more

Father with his son – and the car in which he later killed him.

After struggling to cope with the end of his 10-year marriage to wife Erica, Mr Pedersen killed their two children, Ben, seven, and Freya, six, and then killed himself. The bodies of Ben and Freya Pedersen were found stabbed to death next to their father after he knifed them on Sunday evening. Their father had recently split from his wife, 43. After frenziedly stabbing the children to death in a 'terrifying' attack, Mr Pedersen turned the larger knife on himself and drove it three times into his chest and once into his forearm. Mr Pedersen took the children to a remote country lane in Hampshire where he parked the car. The bodies were found by a dog walker, who saw Mr Pedersen's Saab Convertible and then noticed a child's leg. ¶

Daily Mail

easily recognize our own smouldering tendencies in the demented actions of the bloody protagonists.

7.

MUCH OF THE news is in the end an account of people around the globe, in all sorts of positions, getting things very wrong. They fail to master their emotions, contain their obsessions, judge right from wrong and act decently when there is still time. We shouldn't waste their failures. The news, like literature and history, can serve as that most vital of instruments, a 'life simulator' – which is to say, a machine that inserts us into a variety of scenarios stretching far beyond anything we might ordinarily have to cope with and that affords us a chance safely, and at our leisure, to hone our best responses.

Yet too often the news doesn't help us to learn from the experiences of our wretched brethren; it doesn't actively try to spare us and our societies the full force of error at every new turn. If, as we have already seen, a good life demands that we learn from, and imitate, the example of inspiring figures, it also requires us to undertake close study of those whose behaviour should profoundly scare, horrify and warn us. These are two sides of the same coin of growth and development, and it lies within the remit of the news, if not yet on its agenda, to help us with both.

Accident

A father taking his daughter to school in Derbyshire has been killed after his car skidded into an icy river, only minutes before his wife, on a school run with their son, also crashed into the water. The two children and their mother managed to escape unhurt from the cars but, despite desperate attempts by local residents, the father could not be saved and died in hospital. He had been driving along a bridle path north of the A6 in Derbyshire, when his Toyota Aygo veered off the path and became submerged in the River Wye. ❡

Huffington Post

1.

IT IS, OF course, an appalling story. The dead man was only forty-two; friends remembered him as a 'wonderful, loving father, husband, brother and son'. To shock us further, the news story goes on to give details about the family's frantic struggles in the freezing river; it describes neighbours' failed attempts to rescue the driver from the overturned car; and it reveals the parents' fateful last-minute decision to take this treacherous narrow road rather than their usual (safer, wider) route. It needed just a little patch of black ice for a life to be destroyed. It might so easily have been simply another ordinary morning. The crash dominated the headlines in Britain for several hours one January day (until a plane exploded into flames just after take-off in Nepal).

The disaster belongs to a second, equally compelling and popular category of bad news which is distinct from tragedy in that here there is no one in particular to blame. The causes of calamity lie not with any psychological factors or disturbances within the minds of the protagonists but simply with our species' vulnerability to mishap, with the extreme fragility of our constitution and the unpredictability of nature. We are reminded that we are only ever a rogue spark, a tenacious germ, a loose tile or a strong gust of wind away from the end.

2.

ONCE AGAIN, THE surface paradox is why we should be so interested in these stories of accident, when it might be logical to presume that we would more naturally be nourished by happier tales; that courage to continue with our own lives would best be fostered by exposure to the positive and resilient aspects of experience.

Though the benefits of good news may be obvious when it comes to our own lives, they clearly don't apply when it comes to hearing about others'. There is a peculiar, though undeniable, benefit to be found in exposure to the sufferings of strangers.

This may be because we are all, somewhere within us, uncomfortably sad and disappointed. We harbour, quietly, a lot of darkness. At the same time, we live in societies that ceaselessly promote images of ambition and happiness, of thriving relationships, lucrative careers and successful endeavours, most of which lie painfully out of our reach.

It is the persecutory impact of these images of fulfilment that news of disasters helps to alleviate. The crashes, cancers, explosions and fires relativize our own failures. Disaster bears within it a broad and helpful message: *humanity suffers*. It is this moral that our unconscious apprehends and applies to the particulars of our own griefs (which may be nothing graver than the rejection of a business proposal or a slight to our ego dealt out by an enemy). The differences in proportion between our difficulties and the accident victim's may seem obscene, but they are also (privately) supremely useful. The exaggerated scale of the pain that someone else has to endure serves to put our problems in perspective. We stand to feel a new gratitude for certain basic privileges that we lost sight of in our envious or frustrated moods. Whatever our disappointments, we have not just had a relative die in a car crash, we have so far avoided contracting a fatal virus and our house is still standing. Immersing ourselves in accounts of misfortune can enable us to adopt a more constructive and generous attitude towards ourselves and others. The growth of tolerance and a measure of hope may paradoxically be fed by news of extreme sorrow.

3.

HORRIFIC ACCIDENTS SIMULTANEOUSLY serve a refocusing function. Most of what upsets us from day to day is disconnected from what ultimately gives our life its meaning – and yet these stresses absorb our energies with vicious intensity nevertheless. Vivid reminders of mortality call our prosaic obsessions into question. When measured against our limited timespans, the true insignificance of some of our concerns is emphasized and our narcissistic, frivolous tendencies can cede to our more sincere and purposeful sides.

News of accidents humbles us into acknowledging that, if life is as fragile as this, if we really have no guarantee that there are decades left ahead, then we don't want to be people who spent an afternoon arguing with a beloved, who refused to forgive a friend for a minor transgression or who neglected a genuine talent in favour of an unhappy sinecure. The thought of death has the power to rearrange our priorities, returning to the surface the more valuable parts of us which have a tendency to get submerged in the everyday struggles. Evidence of what there is really to fear has the chance to scare us into leading our lives as we know, in the core of our being, that we properly should.

The notion that the thought of death should be able to restore meaning to our lives has a long history. For centuries in Europe, the studies and bedchambers of the powerful were routinely

Philippe de Champaigne, *Vanitas*, c. 1663.

Woman Killed Instantly by Falling Tree Branch

A New Zealand-born accounts manager, Erena Wilson, received 'non-survival head injuries' after being hit by a Lebanese cedar branch blown off by a gust of wind in the Royal Botanical Gardens in Kew, south-west London, on Sunday. She was walking through the popular tourist attraction with two friends when she was suddenly struck. The friends of the 31-year-old described hearing a loud 'crack' before realising a branch was falling. They fled but when they looked behind, they saw Miss Wilson lying on the ground. Despite paramedics battling to save her, she was pronounced dead at the scene. Her family said they were 'very saddened'. Her colleagues paid tribute to a 'star' with a bright future ahead of her. 'It is difficult to put into words how we all feel following the tragic passing of our colleague and friend Erena Wilson,' said Gez Lowry, a Human Resources manager at the company where she worked. ❡

Daily Telegraph

decorated with a human skull, a real or a painted one, which was prominently positioned to catch one's eye and could usefully interrupt one's train of thought as one plotted petty revenge against a rival or prepared to betray a lover.

The news offers us the opportunity to use its grim stories as our own, modern version of these skulls. It would help if these stories could even be laid out under the title 'Vanitas', so that there would be no doubt as to what moral we were meant to draw from them. They would then cease to be merely records of private pain and could instead help us to embark upon the far more important task of living in accordance with our true talents and interests in whatever precious moments we may have left before a falling tree branch calls time on us.

4.

THEN AGAIN, WE should be careful not to let others' dramas work a contrary and less helpful effect on us. Rather than prompting us to focus on our own neglected priorities, these stories can also risk distracting us from our deeper concerns. The scale, colour and immediacy of disasters in the news gives them the power to elbow themselves to the forefront of our consciousness, where they insistently squat, demanding updates every ten minutes (which the news duly obliges us with), thereby obscuring the call of all those far quieter yet for us far more consequential worries which we need to face within ourselves. When a plane has just crashed in Nepal, we may reflexively start to respond in the manner of an air accident investigator or a panicked relative, rather than remember

Nepal Plane Inferno

A plane flying 19 people towards Mount Everest went down in flames on the outskirts of the Nepalese capital Friday, killing everyone on board including seven Britons and five Chinese, police said. The twin-propeller Sita Air plane had just taken off from Kathmandu and was headed to the town of Lukla when it plunged into the banks of a river near the city's airport around daybreak. Witnesses described hearing the screams of passengers and seeing flames coming from one of the plane's wings moments before it hit the ground, while airport authorities said the pilot had reported hitting a bird shortly after take-off. 'We could hear people inside the aircraft screaming, but we couldn't throw water at the plane to put out the fire because we were scared that the engines were about to explode,' said Tulasha Pokharel, a 26-year-old housewife who was one of the first on the scene. ¶

Agence France-Presse

that this is not in fact really any of our business – and that we ought more fairly to be spending the day looking within, trying to interpret those faint pulses of anxiety upon which the effective management of our selves depends.

A balanced life requires a curious combination of inner and outer concern: we have to internalize the general message that emerges from others' accidents – that we are highly fragile and temporary – without, however, getting so deeply immersed in their particulars that we allow the disasters of strangers to become excuses or means by which we avoid our responsibilities to ourselves. We must both register and yet at the same time not fixate upon the sadness and pain with which the news seeks to confront us at every turn.

We are so used to equating being human with the simple act of feeling that we are apt to lose sight of what a necessary achievement it is occasionally to remain numb. Such are the limits of our own concentration and emotional resources, having a serious and appropriate concern for ourselves and the handful of people who deeply depend upon us must frequently involve a calculated restriction of sympathy for, and interest in, others – a due recognition, in other words, not at all psychopathic in nature, that whatever the news may suggest and however immediate, alarming and touching its tales can be, the problems it raises are not always our own.

Nature

Only hours from now, the Tri-State Area will be blanketed by record heavy snow and hit by exceptionally powerful winds. The National Weather Service has issued a blizzard warning for all of New York City, Long Island, northeastern New Jersey, Connecticut and southern Westchester County. Snow accumulations are expected to range from 20 to 24 inches, with the higher amounts north and east of New York City. In many area grocery stores, shelves are bare, with people rushing to stock up on essentials ahead of a super storm that could force them inside for many days. ¶

CBS News

... Rather cloudy and warm, with most places remaining dry overnight but a little light rain or drizzle is still possible, mainly in the east...

We normally pay the weather little attention. It behaves roughly as it should and therefore stays outside of the news itself. It is rare for us even to look up for long. We certainly don't follow the example of John Constable, who for periods between 1821 and 1822 spent several hours each day on the slopes of Hampstead Heath, intently examining the moods of the sky, producing 150 precise and quietly stunning watercolour, crayon and oil studies of the vaporous shapes drifting over his head – in a process of devoted observation he called 'skying'.

Our eyes are instead fixed on the human drama below: who was promoted; where bond prices might be headed; how the budget stand-off was resolved. What is above us in the atmosphere is daily simplified into one or another of those icons beloved of weather forecasters, which, in their naive reductiveness, stand in relation to the subtleties of the sky rather as news reports stand in relation to the complexities of existence.

2.

... The snow storm is right now on its way northeast, threatening 20 states and 160 million residents in its path...

Until the day when nature forces itself upon our distracted attentions through one of its major disruptive events: a tornado, a flood, a blizzard, a tsunami or another kind of localized apocalypse.

John Constable, *Cloud Study*, 1821.

In the case of this snowstorm, the forecasters have the monster well mapped. In the National Weather Center, an IBM Power 7 supercomputer, with a peak processing performance of one petaflop, keeps the glacial spectre firmly within its sights, though the ability to predict what will happen gives the experts no power whatsoever to alter nature's implacable intent.

Seven major airports will be shut down and some 8,000 flights cancelled or delayed. All major highways in the area will be closed. School will be suspended. Power lines will fall.

The governor of New Jersey has appeared on television and called the storm an 'impending catastrophe'. But it won't be only that. It will also have some of the distinctive and not entirely off-putting qualities of a brief war won by one's own side.

3.

... Residents of North Canaan, Connecticut, among them small children, lost power in the early hours and had to be evacuated to a series of nearby motels by the emergency services, where they remain ...

Living is something of an emergency anyway, but our struggles must usually be strenuously concealed. Our anxieties churn away within us, yet on the outside we must smile and deliver upbeat answers to enquiries about how we're doing. The storm calls a temporary end to this charade. With the wind howling outside, we're allowed to be worried and, even more blessedly, we can direct our worries towards something large, objective and (however odd this might sound to the patrol crews who are out gritting the roads) relatively *simple* – for it is ultimately easier to dig, rescue, save and resuscitate than to meet the challenges of those quieter, more temperate days when we are left alone to bear the responsibilities of making a living, staying in love, raising sane children and not wasting our brief lives.

The storm helps us to reconnect with other people too. At normal times, we can't presume what is on their minds, but now we have a ready-made point of connection and communion with just about anyone. Normally our impressions of what other people are like, largely formed by news bulletins, can inspire the conclusion that everyone must be either a murderer or a paedophile, but in the storm it hardly seems that way; in fact, they show a proclivity for swaddling shivering dogs, serving soup to the stranded and pushing strangers' SUVs out of snowdrifts. Against the backdrop of miles of polar whiteness, the value of any fellow human is thrown into relief. Criteria for compatibility drop to the modest level at which they should perhaps always have been. As when we are drunk, it feels as though we could love anyone.

4.

… Some of the strongest snow falls were reported near Allegheny National Forest and in the area around DuBois and Slippery Rock …

There is poetry in the names of distant parts of the country which we have never been to nor perhaps even suspected existed. Naive artworks spring to mind, depicting remote homesteads, water towers, painted barns – an older way of life in which people know about livestock and flowers and taking their time; rebukes to our ignorant, technologically overconfident city ways.

5.

... Officials announced that the whiteout conditions had forced the airport to shut down completely. Earlier, conditions had reduced air traffic to a single runway, but maintenance workers were having trouble seeing each other through the blinding snow.

Everything is upside down. Aircraft that normally soar to 35,000 feet now sit idle in serried ranks, immobilized under heavy coats of snow. A pilot makes a show of trying to dig out an Airbus A320 with a shovel. The power goes out in the headquarters of an insurance firm and the otherwise sober employees head outside to make snowmen. After the pipes freeze at a chic hotel, the guests exchange the isolated luxury of their rooms for the brightly lit conviviality of a nearby ice rink.

Nature puts us all in our places. Being made to feel small isn't something we welcome when it's done to us by another person, but to be apprised of our essential nothingness by something so much greater than ourselves is in no sense humiliating. Our egos, exhaustingly aware of every slight they receive and prone relentlessly to compare their advantages with those enjoyed by others, may even be relieved to find themselves finally humbled by forces so much more powerful than any human being could ever muster.

In former times, we would be put in our places by the threat of the divine. The gods would quench our hubris and in thunderous voices remind us not to exceed our stations. In a largely secular age, however, it falls to nature, and in particular to so-called 'bad weather', to take up this role and to the news to spread the word. It is the isobars and cold fronts that remind us that – for all our clever machines and ingenious ways – we are still weak and must learn at times simply to surrender to events. We fret and complain, but have no option other than to succumb to an enforced meteorological Sabbath.

Across the eastern seaboard, the mobile masts are down, the power is out, the trucks are stranded, the supermarkets are closed, snow is falling over Central Park and adding another layer to the pines in Mohawk Forest. It is a disaster, a calamity, the worst storm in a generation: the news isn't lying about that. But it might add, this disaster is a lesson in wisdom, too. Tidy modern technological society, marked by its constant competitive solipsism, has done most of us sufficient harm that we may not mind so very much when, for a time at least, it gets a little roughed up by nature's awesomely indifferent hand.

Health News

Green tea and red wine have long been touted as possible weapons against cancer, now new evidence shows that compounds in both may help fend off Alzheimer's disease. University researchers have found that natural chemicals – EGCG in green tea and resveratrol in red wine – may disrupt a key step of the Alzheimer's disease pathway. Researchers were able to interrupt a process that allows harmful clumps of proteins to latch onto brain cells using purified extracts of EGCG and resveratrol. ❡

CTV News

1.

WHILE MOST OF its energy is devoted to briefing us about the gruesome ways in which various individuals have recently met their end, in the area that it terms 'health', the news takes on a very different project. Here it collects information to assist us in the task of living for a very long time or possibly even, though it doesn't ever come out and say this directly, forever. It introduces us to scientists who are permanently poised to reinvent existence. They are busy inventing microscopic robots that will travel through our veins; synthesizing drugs to regulate our moods; mapping our genes; cloning our organs and limbs; and reassessing the life-and-death-giving nature of everyday foodstuffs and medicines, especially wine, olive oil and aspirin.

2.

TO LIVE IN modernity – an era contemporaneous with the triumph of the news – is to be constantly reminded that, thanks to science and technology, change and improvement are continuous and relentless. This is part of the reason we must keep checking the news in the first place: we might at any moment be informed of some extraordinary development that will fundamentally alter reality. Time is an arrow following a precarious, rapid and yet tantalizingly upward trajectory.

In pre-modern societies, by contrast, people thought of time as a wheel. Life was ineluctably cyclical. The most important truths were recurring; the cycle could not be avoided or broken. Even if having regular access to news had been technologically possible, it wouldn't have been very psychologically necessary. Societies that see time as a wheel rather than an arrow feel no pressing need to check the headlines every quarter of an hour.

3.

WE ARE MORE impatient – and optimistic about the future. The underlying, unmentioned promise of health news is that science might one day discover a cure for everything, death included.

It might be simpler if this unspoken claim were categorically untrue. The reality is more complicated. We will one day, perhaps in 780 years' time, crack the mysteries of ageing and disease. But it will be too late for you and me. The fundamentals of our lives are fated to adhere to the same cycle known to all our ancestors.

Despite its general interest in the macabre, the news refuses to be grim or dark enough in its reporting on 'health'-related matters. It continues to treat the latest findings about red wine, gene therapy and the benefits of eating walnuts with a superstitious reverence not dissimilar to that which might once have inspired a devout Catholic pilgrim to touch the shin bone of Mary Magdalene – in the hope of thereby securing ongoing divine protection. Rather than face up squarely to the unqualified inevitability of decay, the news prefers to flog the newly discovered health advantages of drinking grapefruit juice and wearing tight cotton socks on long-haul plane journeys.

Amidst its appetite for murders and explosions, the news remains unhelpfully squeamish with regard to ordinary mortality.

Its proclivity for turning death into a climactic spectacle dissuades us from accepting it as a daily reality. We are whisked from the bomb site to the smouldering plane crash; we are rarely shown the everyday business of an octogenarian heart giving out.

Before they were displaced in our consciousness by the news, religions placed the task of preparing us for death at the heart of their collective missions. The needs and fears that we once brought to our places of worship have not disappeared in the secular age: we remain tormented by anxiety and a longing for comfort in relation to mortality. But these emotions receive little public acknowledgement, being left instead to haunt us in the small hours, while in the more practical and functional parts of the day the news keeps drawing our attention, with deranged zeal, to the newly discovered anticarcinogenic properties of blueberries and a daily teaspoonful of walnut oil.

VII

Consumption

Dining, Travel, Technology...

The chopped liver on crostini had a wintery smokiness to it, as did a fold of flat bread, scorched on a griddle to black in places, then layered with slices of garlicky wild mushrooms. Best was a fritto misto of squid, anchovies and prawns in batter ... As the chef here used to cook at nearby Bocca di Lupo, it was no surprise that the crumbly, coarse Cotechino sausage with braised cabbage and mustard was outstanding. ¶

Observer

1.

THE NEWS IS intimately connected with the workings of 'consumer society'. Every day a not inconsiderable part of its output is taken up with informing us about objects and services that fall within categories such as Dining, Travel, Technology, Fashion, Motoring and Home Furnishings. The news wants to be helpful here, to spare us mistakes and to assist us in making wiser and more fulfilling purchases.

There is a lot of disapproval in certain quarters about our desire to consume. The modern appetite for acquiring things far and above what is strictly necessary to survive is frequently described as shallow, destructive of the planet, futile, greedy and, in a word that rolls all these insults into one, *materialistic*.

Yet given just how great a share of our societies' resources is taken up with the manufacture and sale of non-essential goods, it may be no frivolous task to try to ensure that our acts of consumption proceed as well as they possibly can. The news has a serious job to do in helping us to spend our money well.

2.

IN FULFILLING ITS self-imposed brief, the news tends to examine and report on three things: first, what is available on the market; second, what it costs; and third, whether or not it is any good.

To these ends, it will dispatch journalists to the restaurant to try the pear, Gorgonzola and chicory salad; to the hotel to evaluate the all-inclusive spa weekend, and to the consumer electronics fair to scrutinize the new smartphone's browser and camera.

Whole sea bream, under review.

These are surely important matters, yet to restrict consumer news to such practical investigations is to overlook a key feature of why we are motivated to buy certain things in the first place. The kinds of purchases surveyed in the news generally sit well beyond necessity. In acquiring them, what we are after is rarely solely or even chiefly just material satisfaction; we are also guided by a deeper, often unconscious desire for some form of psychological transformation. We don't only want to *own* things; we want to be *changed* through our ownership of them. Once we examine consumer behaviour with sufficient attention and generosity, it becomes clear that we aren't indelibly materialistic at all. What makes our age distinctive is our ambition to try to accomplish a variety of complex psychological goals via the acquisition of material goods.

3.

Few dishes are as satisfying and elemental as a simply grilled sea bream, served at a plain wooden table with checked napkin and chunky scuffed cutlery. The flesh had just the right consistency, with no additions beyond a little flaky sea salt, some finely chopped parsley and a dash of lemon...

Our ostensible reason for wanting to travel to the new restaurant in the centre of town is that we feel like having a bite to eat. But a substantial, perhaps even decisive part of our desire has a less mundane, more subtly psychological basis: we want to absorb the values of the restaurant itself. We want (in some vague sense) to *become like it*: Relaxed, Dignified, Convivial, Content with Simplicity, In Touch with Nature, At Ease with Others. These are the abstract virtues that we semiconsciously detect in the dishes, the service and the decor, and which we are confusedly seeking to bolster in ourselves through the ingestion of a sea bream with chopped parsley and a side order of burrata with lentils and basil oil.

Each of the 82 rooms gives out onto the azure sea in the bay. In front of the hotel is a large, quiet pool, on the surface of which the gardener scatters flowers early every morning. The air is balmy, the breeze ideally gentle...

Likewise, we don't want merely to visit a calm and tranquil hotel for a few days; we are in search, rather, of a physical environment that can assist us in a larger project of becoming Calm and Tranquil people. We go abroad not just for a change of scenery but in the hope that the outer landscape will help to rearrange the inner one.

The smartphone sends data at dizzying speeds, can take pin-sharp images, understands voice commands and could hold your entire library in its prodigious memory...

And by a similar logic, we don't want the phone only for practical reasons; we also want to assume some of its traits, we want to grow a little more Rational, Elegant, Capable and Precise.

4.

GIVEN THAT CONSUMPTION is a far more complicated – and interesting – process than it first appears, consumer news should re-examine its underlying assumptions about the needs of its audiences.

We are currently accustomed to being guided as to what we might buy under headings such as:

DINING

TRAVEL

TECHNOLOGY

FASHION

But a fairer and richer assessment of our needs would group consumer news stories under rather different headings:

CONVIVIALITY

CALM

RESILIENCE

RATIONALITY

Restaurants, trips abroad and electronic equipment may well give rise to desires, but it is misleading to suggest that they are our ultimate aims. They are merely subsidiaries of larger psychological objectives upon which the investigations of consumer journalism should properly focus.

5.

THE IDEAL CONSUMER news of the future would not be opposed to the material realm. Although some schools of thought have argued that materialism of any kind should play no role whatever in a decent life, the truth is more complex. Material objects are promises of, and enticements to, future states of mind; they provide us with idealized images of where we want to get to. The diminutive Italian city car speaks of a winning cheekiness and playfulness, the titanium desk lamp hints at a busy life reduced to its meaningful essence, the mountain hiking holiday promises an end to hesitancy and fragility and the birth of a new and more resilient self.

Purchasing any of these items won't on its own grant us a more secure hold on the inner states that they speak of. But these items can provide us with an inspiring picture of a destination and thereby bolster our efforts to get there. For better and for worse, consumerism is condemned *not* to be a total waste of money.

Religions have always understood this dualism. While trying to influence their believers in spiritual ways, they have simultaneously appreciated the function that might be played in the shaping of character by particular foods, clothes, travels and items of interior decoration. For example, Zen Buddhism advises its adherents not only to read and to pray, but also to furnish their homes with pieces of celadon pottery, which they are directed to contemplate in order to bolster a commitment to Simplicity and Ego-lessness. There is in this recommendation to purchase no hint of the modern Western assumption that a beautiful pot can on its own transform one's character, but at the same time Zen wisely acknowledges that the right sort of pot approached in the right sort of way can make a worthwhile contribution to inner evolution.

In the secular sphere, we can likewise acknowledge that material goods are sometimes able to lend us valuable encouragement – that a new coat may, for instance, give us an inspiring glimpse of a more confident self or that a plain crockery set may goad us towards a calmer demeanour. Yet at the same time we need to bear in mind that the hoped-for transformation won't occur simply through the act of purchase. We need to do our acquiring within the context of a sufficiently multifaceted and subtle assault on the desirable auras that hover around objects.

In the ideal consumer news section, categories like Confidence and Calm would present us with a range of both conceptual and material options. We would learn about psychological approaches we might take to reach a desired destination – listening to a certain piece of music, reading a book about a period of history, studying a school of philosophy or performing a mental exercise – but we would also be shown a number of material purchases in sympathy with our desired outlook – a particular sort of jacket, perhaps, or a trip abroad, or a comfortable armchair.

6.

BECAUSE WE HAVE allowed ourselves to divorce consumption from our deeper needs, our purchases have become unsupportive of our psyches. Just as consumer news has helped to create this schism, it can also help to rectify it, for it is in large measure the media that informs our notions of what we should be buying, and to what end. The categories, language, positioning and cues it uses when presenting options for purchase possess an extraordinary power to influence what we feel we must own and do. By changing something as apparently minor as the categories in which consumer news reports its findings, by focusing on genuine needs rather than inchoate desires, we might start to do proper justice to the underlying aspirations generated by consumer goods – goods that we exhaust ourselves and our planet to make and pay for. We thereby stand a chance of becoming truer versions of what consumer news has always wanted us to be: happy shoppers.

Culture

Spring is upon us, and with it some of the best shows, performances, books and events. Let our critics and writers guide you through some of the highlights of a packed season in architecture, literature, film, art, dance, theater and jazz, classical, pop and country. ¶

Los Angeles Times

1.

WE LIVE IN an era of unparalleled cultural richness. Every year, humanity produces some 30,000 films, 2 million books and 100,000 albums, and 95 million people visit a museum or art gallery.

Given the constraints of time, in this realm like so many others, news outlets have an essential and prestigious role to play in shaping our sense of what we should attend to. It is cultural journalism's task to sift through the torrent of creativity in order to direct us to the best works of art of our time. Cultural journalism is entrusted with nothing less than the brokerage of a set of contented marriages between art and its audiences.

2.

THE PROFESSION OF evaluating and recommending works of art for a living seems straightforward from a distance, but in order to be carried out with any measure of ambition and coherence, it requires a news organization to ask itself a large and notoriously slippery question: 'What is art actually for?'

The modern world tends towards unanimous agreement that art is extremely important, something close to the meaning of life. The trappings of this elevated regard include considerable state and private resources devoted to its funding, countless individual sacrifices made in its name and a vast amount of attention accorded it in public and private life.

Despite this esteem, the reasons behind art's special status tend to be assumed rather than explicitly explained. Its value is taken to be a matter of common sense. To ask why we should bother to read books, listen to music or admire paintings is to risk sounding either impudent or pedantically stuck on one of those questions to which all clever people seem to have secured satisfying answers long ago.

Yet it shouldn't be possible to describe the latest film as a 'must-see' or a new book as a 'masterpiece' in the absence of a well-reasoned thesis – and one, moreover, somewhere clearly articulated – about the purpose of art.

3.

ONE POSSIBLE THEORY runs like this: art (which here is taken to include literature, music, film, theatre and the visual arts) is a therapeutic medium that helps to guide, exhort and console its audiences, assisting them in evolving into better versions of themselves.

Art is a tool to help us with a number of psychological frailties which we would otherwise have trouble handling: our inability to understand ourselves, to laugh sagely at our faults, to empathize with and forgive others, to accept the inevitability of suffering without falling prey to a sense of persecution, to remain tolerably hopeful, to appreciate the beauty of the everyday and to prepare adequately for death.

In relation to such flaws and many others, art delivers its healing powers, offering us, for example, a poetry book that delincates an emotion we had long felt but never understood, a comedy that shakes us from self-righteous indignation, an album that gives us a soundtrack of hope, a play that turns horror into tragedy, a film that charts a saner path through the difficulties of love or a painting that invites us to a more gracious acceptance of age and disease.

4.

THIS EXPLICITLY THERAPEUTIC theory of art in turn hints at a purpose for cultural journalism: that it should direct our lonely, confused, scared and stricken souls to those works of culture most likely to help us to survive and thrive.

The cultural journalist should act as a kind of chemist, picking out from among the myriad of available works those most likely to be able to help their audiences with their inner travails, treating the storehouse of art as if it were a gigantic pharmacy.

At the end of reviews, one might find discrete tags, comparable to the labels on pill packets, that would specify what sort of situation a given work might be *for* – and why. Reviewers would realize the importance of orientating their analyses in relation to the inner lives of their putative audiences and would deliver their verdicts as versions of psychological prescriptions.

A therapeutic approach to cultural journalism would increase the number of occasions when moments of personal difficulty could be assuaged by art, moments when we had the right novel to help us over an emotional trauma, the right painting to restore a sense of calm, the right film to pull us out of a mood of negativity or frivolity – and a corresponding decrease in the still strikingly high number of times when (despite the millions of artworks in existence) we nevertheless find ourselves with nothing in particular that it feels resonant for us to read, to listen to or to see.

Assisted by a more ambitious cultural journalism, we might at key moments have a new capacity to be a little less mean and unhappy.

5.

THAT WE SHOULD have problems finding our way to the necessary works of art is both peculiar and poignant when, ostensibly, we have never had better access to culture. We pride ourselves on the technological inventions that have made millions of books, films and images available to us almost instantaneously and often at low cost. But access to a dizzying range of works turns out to be very different from knowing which of these works might be right for us. We have up until now done everything to make art available; we are still at the dawn of knowing how to unite people with the works that stand the best chance of mattering to them.

Journalism is in part to blame for this disjuncture for it sits at the head of the sluice of culture. Here, as in many other areas, the information it presents to us can be confusingly random, because journalists are prone to define their reporting priorities not according to any well-thought-out psychological agenda, but in deference to the promotional calendar of the publishing, film and museum industries. Review pages end up dominated by bestseller lists or charts of cinema attendances, as though popularity alone might be the most productive criteria by which to decide on what to read or see next.

Furthermore, an unhelpful amount of cultural journalism is dedicated to attacking works of art that critics deem substandard. Though this may be a diverting spectator sport, it has little to do with the more useful mission of trying to unite a time-short and suffering audience with works that would be of genuine benefit to them. It hardly seems a wise expenditure of effort to inform the public of works of art whose existence it had heretofore never suspected, only then to insist – often with considerable brio – that they should ignore them completely.

In any case, a work may be legitimately worthy and still not resonate, should we encounter it at the wrong moment for *us*. We can end up in the company of a 'great' book, film or exhibition whose merits we objectively recognize, but which nevertheless leaves us cold, bored and guilty – because critics have not sufficiently or subtly specified, as good pharmacists should, for what condition the work might be a fit corrective. An awkward truth is that a large, even critical, part of the possible value of any work of art depends on the psychological situation of its audiences. Art can only come truly alive on those precious occasions when its content is in sync with an inner need – occasions that cultural journalism should train its intelligence upon trying to identify and make known, taking on the role of the dispensing pharmacist of mankind's most powerful therapeutic medicine.

VIII.

Conclusion

Personalization

You can manually control many elements of Google News. The central place for your customization settings can be found by clicking on the 'Personalize your news' button, which appears as a gear icon in the top right corner of the Google News homepage. In these settings you can adjust how much you prefer to see of news from a given section by adjusting the slider toward the plus sign (+), or the minus sign (–). ¶

Google News

I.

THERE WAS ONCE a time when we consumed all that we were given of the news – thirty pages of a paper or half an hour of a bulletin – and trusted that those in charge of providing it had more or less accurately captured the most significant events of the world within the means available. Technology has taught us otherwise. We are now conscious that the supply of news is almost infinite; that every day yields another exabyte of images and words, and that newspapers and news bulletins are in truth thimblefuls of information arbitrarily pulled out of a boundless ocean of data by hard-pressed editors, daily forced to do no better than guess at the desires of a putative 'average reader'.

Inevitably, they don't always get it right. They may go on too long about a West African war or an incomprehensible debt repayment scheme. They may update us against our will about a society wedding or a Caribbean hurricane. We may feel as if we were being force-fed entrées we never ordered.

But it won't necessarily always go on like this. Technology promises to give us the power to tell our computers about our tastes and then have them automatically sift through the day's offerings to present us with bulletins precisely tailored to our personalities. No longer will the supply of news be dictated only by the sometimes wrong-headed assumptions of editors. We will have achieved an individualistic Utopia: a world with as many varied news channels in it as there are audience members.

2.

YET THE PROSPECT of giving up on objective editorial direction has its alarming aspects, for it begs the question of how well equipped most of us really are to know what sort of news we need to be confronted by.

The ambition of living a good adult life in a modern democracy requires that we take on board all kinds of knowledge to help us to remain moral, self-aware and safe and to assist us in discharging our public and private responsibilities effectively. Yet some of this knowledge may not seem especially appealing at first sight. Left in charge of programming our own news, we risk cutting ourselves off from information that might be deeply important to our evolution. Far from helping us to develop a rich and complex individuality, 'personalized news' might end up aggravating our pathologies and condemning us to mediocrity.

Imagine how personalization would have worked for, say, Marie Antoinette – someone temperamentally squeamish about distressing Political news and who would have been drawn to turning up the dial on Fashion and Entertainment. Word that 5,000 of her subjects were starving in Rennes might have been sacrificed to an exhaustive report on the dresses sported by guests at a party given by the Duchesse de Polignac – an ordering of priorities that would have revealed itself as a problem only by October 1793, as the queen awaited her fate on the guillotine steps.

Or picture a man with a strong desire to avoid feeling envy, empowered by new technology to choke off the supply of any news about successful people. Pleased though he might be at having freed himself from what he termed 'silly stories', he might also miss some critical if uncomfortable clues as to his own development and future direction.

Equally blinkered in a different way, another person might want to hear of nothing but tragedy in the underdeveloped world. But what if this exclusive attention to tales of starvation and butchery were being used as a noble but emotionally convenient excuse for not expressing affection towards better-fed but more demanding people closer to home?

Personalization would be an improvement over the current editorial system if, and only if, users had a highly mature and complex sense of what sort of news they needed to hear. But this would require them, before they could be let anywhere near the dashboard used to program the news-stream, to get to know their own souls extremely well. Only after extensive self-examination, perhaps with the help of a psychoanalyst, would they be adequately prepared to set the dials on their personal news engines, aware of the sorts of stories that were needed to challenge their defences, expand their horizons and excite in them the right sort of envy. Like all gateways to increased freedom of choice, the prospect of personalized news serves only to highlight the difficulties of choosing wisely.

3.

THE ISSUE OF personalization returns us to a question that informs much of this book: What should the news ideally be? What are the deep needs to which it should cater? How could it optimally enrich us?

We have examined six types of news to try to define what sort of role they might play for us:

Political News
In the face of all the distractions and confusions thrown at us, political news should elicit our interest in the complex mechanics of our societies, help us to agitate intelligently for their reform and accept certain obdurate limitations without fury. Political news should create a rounded, tolerable nation in the imagination of its audience, allowing for moments of pride and collective sympathy. It should monitor not just those in power but all the systemic ills that hold back the community, while additionally recognizing its own momentous capacity to influence the values of the nation it comments on.

World News
This subspeciality should open our eyes to the nature of life in foreign countries above and beyond their moments of bloodthirsty and dramatic crisis, which paradoxically block our capacities for empathy and identification. It should set aside its obsession with neutral reporting in order to give us rich, sensory and intermittently personal portraits of other nations. It should, by appropriating some of the techniques of travel literature and by constant recourse to great photo journalism, help us to humanize the Other in our minds, shaking us out of our globalized provincialism.

Economic News
Ideally, this genre would not only illuminate current economic developments but also investigate the many intelligent and workable

theoretical approaches which could effect saner, more fulfilling versions of market capitalism, thereby quashing both our unnecessary cynicism and our immature rage. It would at the same time represent the activities of businesses in terms that stretched beyond the cold economic data required by investors. It would evoke the human realities that lie beneath our products so as to prompt helpful feelings of gratitude, righteous anger, guilt and awe.

Celebrity News

In this category, we would be introduced to some of the most admirable people of our era – as judged by mature and subtle criteria – and guided as to how we might draw inspiration and advice from them. The famous would make us envious in productive and measured ways, helping us to realize our own genuine but timid talents by the example of their audacity and perseverance. But we would also be reminded that the best cure for a longing for fame would ultimately be a world in which kindness and respect were more generously and evenly distributed.

Disaster News

The tragedies of others should remind us how close we ourselves often are to behaving in amoral, blinkered or violent ways. Seeing the consequences of such impulses harrowingly played out in the lives of strangers should leave us feeling at once scared and sympathetic rather than hubristic and self-righteous. For their part, the accidents that every day cut down our fellow human beings should demonstrate to us how exposed we constantly are to the risk of sudden death and injury, and therefore make clear with what gratitude and generosity we should greet every pain-free hour.

Consumer News

This field of journalism should alert us to how complicated it is, within an aggressively commercial society, to generate genuine happiness by spending money. It should strive therefore deftly to direct us to those objects and services (and, just as important, those manoeuvres of mind) which stand the best chance of answering our underlying aspirations for a fulfilled existence.

4.

BUT EVEN IF, by a succession of miracles, the news managed one day to do all of the above reliably, we would still retain a handful of reasons for ongoing caution ...

News from Inside

If we read of one man robbed, or murdered, or killed by accident, or one house burned, or one vessel wrecked, or one steamboat blown up, or one cow run over on the Western Railroad, or one mad dog killed, or one lot of grasshoppers in the winter – we never need read of another ... As for England, almost the last significant scrap of news from that quarter was the revolution of 1649; and if you have learned the history of her crops for an average year, you never need attend to that thing again, unless your speculations are of a merely pecuniary character. If one may judge who rarely looks into the newspapers, nothing new does ever happen in foreign parts, a French revolution not excepted. ¶

Henry David Thoreau, *Walden*, 1854

1.

WE EVOLVED FROM humans who lived in societies where not much ever changed – and where any change that did occur was liable to be very significant, and perhaps life-threatening. From this background, we have inherited a cognitive frailty as regards novelty: we immediately suppose that the new must also be the important.

It isn't always. Sanity in a news-dominated age requires us to see that the categories of novelty and importance are overlapping – yet crucially distinct.

When we are feeling edgy and inclined to escape ourselves, what better, more immersive and more *respectable* solution than to run to the news. It provides the ideal, serious-minded excuse for failing to pay attention to many things that might matter more than it does. We willingly give up all responsibilities to ourselves in order to hear of such large and pressing issues as Brazil's debt, Australia's new leader, child mortality rates in Benin, deforestation in Siberia and a triple murder in Cleveland.

2.

IN ITS SCALE and ubiquity, the contemporary news machine can crush our capacity for independent thought. In the European control room of one global news organization, one finds close to 500 people sitting in a gigantic dimly lit concrete atrium decorated with screens and bulletin boards connected by fibre-optic tendrils to every corner of the world. More data flows into the building in a single day than mankind as a whole would have generated in the twenty-three centuries between the death of Socrates and the invention of the telephone. Down the wires come accounts of earthquakes in Guatemala and murders in Congo, profit warnings in Helsinki and explosions in Ankara. There are stories on every conceivable topic and geographical region: on the elections in Burkina Faso and child mortality in Vietnam, on Canadian agricultural subsidies and Rio Tinto's African strategy, on Prada's autumn collection and dim sum restaurants in Zurich. Clocks reveal that it is just after lunch in Khartoum but still early morning in La Paz. It feels like the departure area of a large international airport, affording one something of the same heady sense that one has left behind everything local, rooted and slow-moving and entered into a frenzied, weightless, global realm. Here we are firmly in the modern era, a time of disorientation and randomness in which, thanks to new technologies, we have surrendered our provincial attachments, abandoned the rhythms of nature and, within vast cities, become vividly aware of the simultaneous existence of millions of our demented fellow creatures, all burdened with their particular blend of misfortunes, ambitions and peculiarities.

The pace of the news cycle is relentless. However momentous yesterday's news – the landslides, the discovery of a young girl's half-concealed body, the humiliation of a once-powerful politician – every morning, the whole cacophony begins afresh. The news hub has the institutional amnesia of a hospital's accident and emergency department: nightly the bloodstains are wiped away and the memories of the dead erased.

One wonders whether the torrent of stories could ever momentarily be made to dry up; whether – by an extraordinary effort of coordination – mankind might agree to behave so cautiously that, for a day, there would end up simply being no news. Murderers the world over might delay their intentions, foolhardy swimmers would remain ashore, adulterous politicians would fix their attentions on the lawn. But the overseers of the news need never fear such scarcity. Statistics will assure them that by the end of any twenty-four-hour period, 3,000 people will unwittingly have lost their lives on the world's roads, forty-five people will have been murdered across the United States and 400 fires will have broken out in homes across southern Europe – quite aside from any new and unforeseen innovations in the fields of maiming, terrorizing, stealing and exploding.

3.

IT IS NEVER easy to be introspective. There are countless difficult truths lurking within us that investigation threatens to dislodge. It is when we are incubating particularly awkward but potentially vital ideas that we tend to feel most desperate to avoid looking inside. And that is when the news grabs us.

We should be aware of how jealous an adversary of inner examination it is – and how much further it wishes to go in this direction. Its purveyors want to put screens on our seat-backs, receivers in our watches and phones in our minds, so as to ensure that we will be always connected, always aware of what is happening; never alone.

But we will have nothing substantial to offer anyone else so long as we have not first mastered the art of being patient midwives to our own thoughts.

We need long train journeys on which we have no wireless signal and nothing to read, where our carriage is mostly empty, where the views are expansive and where the only sounds are those made by the wheels as they click against the rails in rhythmical succession. We need plane journeys when we have a window seat and nothing else to focus on for two or three hours but the tops of clouds and the constant presence, only metres away in the inconceivable cold, of a Rolls-Royce engine, slung under the broad ash-grey wing, its discipline and bravery helping to propel our own vagabond thoughts.

4.

WE CAN'T FIND everything we need to round out our humanity in the present. There are attitudes, ideologies, modalities of feeling and philosophies of mind for which we must journey backwards across the centuries, through the corridors of reference libraries, past forgotten museum cabinets filled with rusting suits of medieval armour, along the pages of second-hand books marked with the annotations of their now-deceased owners or up to the altars of half-ruined and moss-covered temples. We need to balance contact with the ever-changing pixels on our screens with the pages of heavy hardback books that proclaim, through their bindings and their typefaces, that they have something to say that will still deserve a place in our thoughts tomorrow.

5.

WE NEED RELIEF from the news-fuelled impression that we are living in an age of unparalleled importance, with our wars, our debts, our riots, our missing children, our after-premiere parties, our IPOs and our rogue missiles. We need, on occasion, to be able to rise up into space in our imagination, many kilometres above the mantle of the earth, to a place where that particular conference and this particular epidemic, that new phone and this shocking wildfire, will lose a little of their power to affect us – and where even the most intractable problems will seem to dissolve against the aeons of time to which the view of other galaxies attests.

6.

WE SHOULD AT times forgo our own news in order to pick up on the far stranger, more wondrous headlines of those less eloquent species that surround us: kestrels and snow geese, spider beetles and black-faced leafhoppers, lemurs and small children – all creatures usefully uninterested in our own melodramas; counterweights to our anxieties and self-absorption.

A flourishing life requires a capacity to recognize the times when the news no longer has anything original or important to teach us; periods when we should refuse imaginative connection with strangers, when we must leave the business of governing, triumphing, failing, creating or killing to others, in the knowledge that we have our own objectives to honour in the brief time still allotted to us.

Picture Credits

Akg-images/Erich Lessing: 194 (bottom); akg-images/Pirozzi: 160 (top right); Alamy/View Pictures: 47; Bridgeman Art Library/De Agostini: 160 (bottom); Bridgeman/Louvre, Paris: 160 (top left); Bridgeman/Musée de la Tesse, Le Mans: 206; Bridgeman/Musée du Petit-Palais, Paris: 112 (bottom); Bridgeman/Musées Royaux des Beaux-Arts de Belgique, Brussels: 106, 108; Bridgeman/National Gallery, London: 25; Bridgeman/Royal Geographical Society, London: 98; Bridgeman/Yale Center for British Art, Paul Mellon Collection, New Haven: 212; © Edward Burtynsky, courtesy Nicholas Metivier Gallery, Toronto/Flowers, London/Paul Kuhn, Calgary: 148 (Detail from the diptych *10 ab*); Cascade News, Manchester: 194 (top); Corbis: 158, 217; Getty Images: 110; © Jacqueline Hassink: 147 (from *The Table of Power (1993–5)*, 6 December 1994); Nico Hogg: 36 (bottom); INS News Agency, Reading: 200 (left); © KIK-IRPA, Brussels: 162 (bottom right); © Magnum Photos/Stuart Franklin: 102 (top & bottom), 104, 118–19; PA Photos: 50, 60, 89 (top), 116–17, 200 (right), 208; Benedict Redgrove/Wired © The Condé Nast Publications Ltd: 150; Carol Rosegg/Shakespeare Theatre Company, Washington, DC: 89 (bottom); Ross Parry Agency, West Yorkshire: 202; David Shankbone: 136; Shutterstock: 36 (top); © Stephanie Sinclair/VII Photo: 114–15; Pete Souza/White House Photo Office: 120–21; Topfoto: 112 (top), 162 (top); Yale University Art Gallery, New Haven: 162 (bottom left); Jenny Zarins: 226 (from *Polpo: A Venetian Cookbook (Of Sorts)* by Russell Norman, Bloomsbury, 2012. Reproduced by kind permission).

Index